Swing Trading Options

The Ultimate Trading Guide to Discover a Safe and Profitable Trading Strategy That Adds Diversity and Rapid Growth to Your Finances and Generates Fast and Secure Profits

Jim Livermore

Table of Contents

Foreword

At one time, trading was exclusive to those who could afford to hire a financial advisor that could facilitate their trades for them or those who could afford the machinery required to get started with trades. The idea of an average person investing in stocks or any sort of financial instrument on the stock market was scarce, as it was not easily accessible to the everyday person.

Since the rise of computers and the internet, many brokerages have taken to developing online platforms that enable everyday people to conduct their own trades. Through tapping into these online platforms, just about anyone can create a strong strategy to earn high profits through their trading activity. As long as you know what you are doing and you are executing the right strategy, you have a great opportunity to earn yourself a higher and more profitable income than you can through just about any other strategy.

It has become my passion to teach other people on how to use the power of these brokerages to their advantage so that they can begin producing their own income through trading. This way, you can skip over the expensive fees and commissions related to working with a full-service brokerage or a financial advisor, and you can become your own secret weapon in trading. You will quickly learn that developing your own skills in trading is the ultimate key to creating success with trade investments.

Through growing your own confidence in trading, you will be able to increase your profitability and decrease your risk in the stock market. Although you cannot completely cancel out the risk, you can certainly decrease it through education, knowledge, and practice.

It is important that you understand right now that trading is, by no means, easy, risk-free, or guaranteed. Despite how much you might prepare and educate yourself, there is always going to be a possibility that things could go wrong. Even professional traders make bad moves from time to time, which result in fairly significant losses to their bottom line.

The key to being successful in your trades, even when losses are happening, is to manage your emotions and stay objective in your positions. The more you learn to balance yourself and stay focused, the better you will come out of every single trade, regardless of how it turns out. Still, we always hope, of course, that it turns out in the best possible way.

Preface

The role of a trader is simple, in theory. The basic role of a trader is to study the market through price charts, identify profitable positions, and buy and sell their way into those positions so that they can earn a profit. Some traders do this with their own capital and with the desire to increase their own income, whereas others do it with the capital of their clients with the desire to increase their clients' income and earn a commission in the process. Either way, they are always scoping out the best positions in the market so that they can trade and capitalize on fluctuations in the prices of financial assets in the market.

If you want to get more specific about how trading works, however, there is a lot more that goes into a trader's role than just that. Traders conduct what is known as *technical analysis,* or carefully constructed reports on how the market is behaving, to identify where the most profitable positions in the market are. They do this by following historical trends and live updates, comparing technical indicators and charts, and paying attention to current news that may impact the direction of the market. Through their analysis, they are primarily looking for the activity of price and volume over time, which enables them to visually represent how a stock is behaving and whether or not it will produce a profitable trade position.

The entire stock market is largely influenced by the emotions of traders, with prices rising when people are greedy and falling when people become afraid. This emotional influence is largely the reason that traders who trade without intense emotional involvement tend to earn the best profits from the market. With that being said, even the best trader will be *influenced* by the emotional forecast of the market, even if they are not being influenced by their own emotions regarding market prices.

A popular trading strategy used by short-term and medium-term traders is known as Swing Trading, which we are going to be talking about right here in this very book. Swing Trading enables people to capitalize on swings in stock prices or the part of the pattern that exists when the market is actively rising or falling. This particular strategy combines the hyperactivity of day trading with the longer profits of positional trading, enabling the trader to maximize their profits over time. By combining swing trading with the financial instrument of options, which are a form of contract, you can increase profitability while also significantly lowering your risk exposure. As a result, you are left with an incredible trade strategy that we are going to spend the next 11 chapters talking about.

In this book, we are going to cover everything you need to know about swing trading options and what you need to do in order to maximize your profits from this unique strategy. This book will serve as a great asset to both new and experienced traders in providing you with plenty of knowledge about how you can leverage this trading strategy.

Jim Livermore

Introduction

Swing Trading Options is a practical, actionable guide to earning profits by executing a swing trading strategy in the options market. I have been studying and using this particular strategy for years to help me increase my profits and hedge myself against risk exposure in the market. Over the years, I have accumulated a large amount of skill and knowledge on how this particular strategy works and what you need to do in order to become a successful swing trader in the options market.

The simple truth is that investing a large amount of time in locating and weaving together different pieces of valuable information from here and there is not the most effective way to learn how to swing trade options. Sure, you might get the information that you need, but it will take far longer than it needs to. To save you the time and trouble, I have designed this all-inclusive guide to help you learn how to swing trade options from start to finish with complete confidence.

As a swing trader, your primary goal will always be to profit from swings in price movements that take place over several days and up to a few weeks. While you might engage in and manage new trades every day, you are not a day trader because you are holding your positions much longer than just a few hours. You might close some trades after a short period of time, but your overall approach will always be looking into the long term so that you can increase your profits.

Swing trading works because you are trading in the direction of the trend, which helps guarantee your profits every single time. You will always wait for the market to pull back before you enter a trade, and you never enter until the stock shows clear signs that it is going to continue in the direction of this trend. This way, you do not enter a short trend and find yourself losing out on profits. This makes following and capitalizing from the trends much easier, resulting in a higher probability of earning profits.

There are several important aspects of swing trading that you will become aware of through this book, including everything from basic trader strategy, such as creating your own schedule and routines, to a more technical strategy, such as specific trading spreads. It is crucial that you know all of this information before you start trading so that you can confidently enter the market and outline strong trade moves for you to make. I strongly recommend you read this book all the way through before using it to help you execute trades. After you have read it all the way through once, you can go back and actively follow the steps to begin engaging in trades. This way, you know exactly what needs to happen at all stages of your trade, and you are already actively protecting yourself against risk in the market.

Chapter 1: What Is Swing Options Trading?

In order to earn money on the stock market, you need to approach it with a specific, simple strategy that is going to enable you to conduct successful trades. Although trading, in and of itself, may seem somewhat complex, especially if you are new to trading, having a specific strategy for how you are going to trade enables you to have a general guideline for every trade you enter. This way, you can feel confident that you are always completing every step of your trade successfully and that things will get easier over time because you are applying the same framework every time.

When you choose to swing trade with options, you are essentially taking an existing trading structure and turning it into your trading strategy. This way, you have a stable guideline to follow that will enable you to make money from each trade by knowing exactly where, when, and how to enter and exit the market. With swing trading, you can capitalize on trades whether the market is bullish (on an uptrend) or bearish (on a downtrend) or even if it is just going sideways. In fact, this versatility is exactly what makes it such a powerful trading strategy since you can generate profits no matter what is happening in the market. After all, your goal when trading is to make money, not to constantly be banking on the future of what might happen with a stock, a sector, or even the economy itself.

What It Means to Swing Trade an Option

If you watch the stock market for any given period of time, you will notice that it moves in what appears to be "waves." These waves portray the stock market alternating between positive and negative positions as it rises and falls in price value.

When it comes to swing trading, you want to capitalize on those waves by identifying when they are about to switch into the opposite direction, which is exactly where you are going to earn your highest profits. In order to make money with swing trading, you want to take your position as soon as a) the market switches into the opposite direction and b) the opposite direction is validated, meaning that it will not immediately switch back. When these two pieces of information are validated, you have found an excellent opportunity to enter on a stock and begin generating income from your investment.

Options themselves are a form of financial instrument that is represented by a contract that affords the investor the *option* to buy the underlying asset being represented by the contract, such as stocks or bonds. If you are selling an option, you are giving the buyer the option to purchase stocks from you, which they will do *if* the stock reaches their favored price point. If they do not, the option will expire worthless, meaning no action will have been taken on it.

If you are buying an option, you are buying the option to purchase stocks from the option writer or the person who is selling the option. Again, you will only exercise your option *if* the stock reaches a desirable price point that results in profit gains. Otherwise, you will let the option expire without worth, or you will sell it to someone else to attempt to recover some of your losses on the cost of the option itself.

Swing trading options essentially means that you are using the strategy of swing trading and applying it to the financial instrument of options. This is beneficial because swing trading itself enables you to earn frequent yet significant profits from your trades. Since you are only holding medium-term positions, you are able to cash-out sooner while also holding on to the position long enough to earn increased profits. It also earns you the reduced risk exposure of options, which comes from the fact that you are buying the option, not the stock, which is significantly cheaper than the stock itself. Still, you do reserve the right to buy the stock should you wish to exercise the option, which means that you guarantee yourself rights to the stock in case the price matches your desired trading point. As a result, you engage in a higher-profit and lower-risk trading style.

How Swing Trading Works (vs. Other Styles)

There are a variety of different strategies that come into play when it comes to trading. The easiest way to break them down is based on the length of the position that you are holding, which ranges from short-term to long-term positions. From there, you can identify different strategies that are applicable to that range, enabling you to find the best trading style for you.

As you have discovered, swing trading is a medium-term trade that lasts a few days up to a couple of weeks. The average swing trade position will not last any longer than about two or three weeks because, at that point, it starts crossing over into long-term trading.

Short-term trading is referred to as day trading because you only intend to hold your position for a few hours and up to a day. If you choose to day trade, your goal will be to offload any stocks you are holding by the end of the day or by the next day at the very latest. If you purchase options and intend to day trade, your options will automatically cancel at the end of the day, which works the same as expiring worthless.

In this case, you will not have an open trade anymore, and you will no longer hold the option to buy the stock that the contract represented. Naturally, day trading can be risky because it can lead to you missing out on profits from your trade positions. Especially if you are not going to be exclusively trading as your career, you can run into a lot of problems securing income this way due to trades expiring or canceling before you have a chance to complete them.

Most day traders trade for a living or have a significant amount of time to invest in trade deals every single day that affords them the opportunity to earn profits this way. Still, it can be risky and does not leave you with much time to earn a significant profit.

Long-term trading is referred to as positional trading, which references the fact that you find a strong position and holding that position for a long period of time. With positional trading, your entire goal is to find a stock that you believe is going to consistently increase in value over time on a bullish market. You will ride out many smaller waves that take place on the day-to-day and week-to-week market, with the intention of the overall month-to-month or year-to-year wave being much larger. In the end, you can earn massive profits, but you will need to be incredibly patient to earn them and eventually cash out on them.

Medium-trading investing through swing trading is often regarded as a happy medium that affords you the quicker profits associated with day trading but over a longer trade duration so that you are not exposed to as much risk. Most people think swing trading is more comparable to day trading due to how long and intense positional trading can be.

The Pros of Swing Trading

The increased opportunities to cash out on profits with a decreased amount of time invested in trade tend to be two of the biggest benefits of swing trading. Many traders who engage in swing trading are able to double, triple, and even quadruple their initial investment in just a few trades by using the best trading strategies possible and staying consistent in their approach. When you combine swing trading with the reduced risks of options, it becomes incredibly simple for you to maximize your profitability and earning potential with swing trading.

Swing trading also tends to be an easier trading strategy as it relies exclusively on technical analysis to identify the best possible trade positions. By creating a strong technical analysis strategy and applying it to every single trade you want to enter, you can validate your positions and step in without much else to it.

Most swing traders have their technical analysis practice down to a fine science that enables them to create a strong case for each trade they are about to make. As a result, they can confidently validate their trades and increase their profitability in minimal timing. We are going to explore how you can make your own technical analysis strategy later on so that you, too, can feel incredibly confident when validating and taking hold of new trade positions.

The Cons of Swing Trading

The downside of swing trading is that you are going to be in markets overnight, and you are not going to be holding long-term positions. This means that you could be subjected to drastic overnight and weekend changes in the market that you might not have enough time to bounce back from due to the shorter duration of the trade.

As a result, you might find that a great trade deal that you were confident in goes sour because of an unexpected change. Unfortunately, this cannot be avoided because the outlook of the economy is constantly changing, and something as simple as a rumor or some unexpected news hitting the headlines can shift everything. While there are things you can do to minimize your losses in this case, including trading options instead of open stocks, there is no way that you can entirely hedge yourself against this risk.

Aside from the uncertainty of the market, another drawback you need to be aware of is that there are generally limited gains that you can achieve with swing trading. Unlike positional trading that capitalizes on massive growth over long periods of time, swing trading exits the market at a specific point, which effectively stops any further growth you may have experienced with that particular trend. Also, because you have gone in with a specific strategy and you have already researched for that specific strategy, it is strongly advised *against* you staying in the market any longer than you anticipated you would.

Staying in the market longer than your strategy outlines to attempt to earn a few extra dollars can expose you to the massive risk and has consistently resulted in massive losses for many traders who were not prepared for what was yet to come. Since you have not researched far enough, and you may not be skilled to conduct the proper research to look that far into the future, you are exposing yourself to huge possible losses. You will need to become okay with exiting the market at an appropriate, pre-determined time in order to minimize your risk, even if that means missing out on further profits.

How to Swing Trade From Home

Conducting your own trade deals is often where the intimidation factor comes in for most people. It seems easy enough to find a full-service brokerage, give them your money, and tell them what you want to happen with your money, including what your risk profile is. At that point, an experienced trader will manage your money and conduct your trades for you. However, this also comes with an increased price tag for the cost of the service ,which may result in lowered profits, and there is no way to guarantee that they are trading with your best interest at heart. For that reason, you really need to learn how you can swing trade from home.

Swing trading from home is not as challenging as you might expect, as you will learn throughout this book. You will need to collect the right tools, such as a proper brokerage and some tools to support you with technical analysis. However, once you are set with the right system at home, you will find that your success largely relies on strategy, strong research, growing knowledge on what you are doing, and a little dash of luck. With these things in place, most of which you will learn about in this book, you can begin confidently trading from the comfort of your own home without paying a single cent more than you have to in order to earn your profits.

Chapter 2: Investment and Trading Opportunities

When you get started with investing, there are various investment and trading opportunities that you can take advantage of to help you increase your profitability. With swing trading, specifically, you are generally paying attention either to options or stocks, as these are the two financial instruments that are going to earn you the best profits with your trading strategy. However, there are other financial instruments available to invest in that can supply you with a larger income by helping you effectively increase your profitability.

In general, there are four specific financial instruments that you should familiarize yourself with as a beginner. While other instruments do exist, these four are the ones that are going to have the greatest impact on your ability to increase profits and earn a stronger income through your investments. Acquainting yourself with them now will help you understand how swing trading options fits into the bigger picture of investments, as well as what other opportunities are available for you to explore at a future date if you so desire.

Stocks

Stocks are what everyone thinks about when they think about trading on the market. Stocks, sometimes called raw stocks, are the actual shares that traders can purchase in a company when they are trading. For example, you could purchase stocks in Apple, which would afford you a certain number of shares in the company. In other words, you would purchase the right to own a very small portion of the company.

Of course, when you invest in stocks and purchase a share of the company, your share will be far too small for you to actually do anything with, in terms of having a say on the board of directors or determining the outlook of the company. However, it is large enough for you to trade and capitalize on, as the value of the company increases.

With swing trading stocks, you are looking for medium-term increases in the evaluation of the company. You want to find companies that are going to experience medium-term increases in the valuation of their shares or their stocks. This regularly happens whenever there is any sort of news impacting the company itself or even when it is just being traded more frequently than other stocks. A great way to identify these stocks, however, is to pay attention to general headlines, as well as stock news platforms as they will give you a greater insight as to what companies are likely going to fluctuate in the near future.

Anything from launching new products to failed product launches or hiring or firing a CEO or senior executive in a company can lead to fluctuation in the price value of these stocks, meaning that they are highly volatile.

For that reason, you need to ensure that you conduct a strong technical analysis before ever engaging in the trade to avoid being subjected to an unexpected and possibly devastating loss. Although there are risk management tools that you can apply to each trade, you want to make sure that you are still incredibly cautious before entering any, as your primary goal is always to maximize your profits, not minimize your losses.

Bonds

To put it simply, a bond is a form of loan that is made to a large organization. As an investor, you invest a certain amount of capital into a bond, and so do several other investors. As a result of your collective investments, a large amount of capital is accumulated that is then borrowed by a company to help them grow their business and, therefore, increase their evaluation. Bonds exist because the sheer size of the entities borrowing require them to borrow from more than one place since one single place could not reasonably invest in the amount that they need. If a bank, for example, were to invest money on something, it would place a massive burden on that bank that would also come with a large risk.

Even if the company was consistently performing well, any changes could result in that company going bankrupt and the bank never receiving their capital back. Instead of the bank taking on such a massive risk, several different investors put up a smaller amount, which decreases each individuals' exposure while also increasing their earning potential. Since such a large amount of capital is being borrowed, it means that the gains on that capital will be massive.

Think about it this way: 2% of 1 million dollars is $20,000, whereas 2% of $1,000 is only $20. Your earning potential in this scenario is much more powerful than your earning potential if you were to invest in something smaller on your own.

When you enter a bond, the organization that is borrowing from you and all of your fellow investors, create a promise to pay the entire loan back by a certain date that is agreed upon by the organization and the investors.

Until then, there are interest payments that are paid out to the investors at a fixed rate until the loan is to be paid back. In this case, you are given back your principal investment or the face value of your investment, as they call it, and you receive back all of the interest, too. As a result, you earn massively through bonds, as long as you are invested in the right companies.

Mutual Funds

Mutual funds are another form of investment that generally requires a long-term position for investing; as you earn more, the longer you are invested in them. The easiest way to understand what a mutual fund is would be to think of it as a basket that is professionally managed by one single individual or company. Despite this, the mutual fund does not have to be invested in through a full-service brokerage; you can still invest manually through your own brokerage and with your own strategy.

The reason why a mutual fund requires a professional portfolio manager is that several people are investing funds into a greater fund that is then allocated into various stocks and bonds and other financial instruments. With the increased amount of cash going into each investment due to everyone trading together, there is an increase in how much can be earned through each investment.

Remember, 2% of one million is a lot higher than 2% of one thousand. This does not necessarily mean that the portfolio manager will be investing in anything worth a million dollars, but it does mean that your earning potential is much higher. In addition, since the fund is managed by a professional and allocated into several different directions, you gain the benefit of diversification, which is a well-known risk management strategy.

For this reason, mutual funds are a great long-term position to enter that will enable you to increase your profits over time.

Options

As you have already come to know, options are a financial instrument that actually represents another financial instrument due to the fact that they are contracts used for trading underlying assets. The entire concept of options might seem confusing if you are new to it, but it does get easier to understand, and it also makes sense as to why they afford you risk-protection while maintaining your profitability.

The easiest way to break down options is to look at them this way. Let's say you see that stock ABC is increasing in value, and you want to invest in it so that you can gain profits form that increasing value. If you were to buy it right now, and it increased in value over the next week, you would sell your stocks and bank your profit. If, however, you were wrong, and the stock actually dropped over the week, you would have lost a percentage of your investment. That percentage might be large, depending on how many shares you had purchased. As a result, you are exposed to greater risk.

Instead of investing directly into stocks, however, you could instead invest in options contracts. These contracts, as you know, afford you the *option* to buy the stock. The options themselves are a lot less of an investment than the stocks themselves, often reflecting only 2-5% of the overall stock value. The investment you make, known as a premium, affords you the opportunity to buy this contract and then hold the right to buy the stock if it turns in your favor. This way, if it does, you can go ahead and purchase the underlying stock and earn your profits. If it doesn't, however, you can let the option expire without worth.

To make options worth it, they come with what is known as a strike price and an expiry date. This strike price reflects the amount that you will pay per share if you choose to buy them, and the expiry date reflects when you have to make your decision by.

If you buy options that are valued less than the increase you expect to see in the market, then you directly purchase your opportunity to increase your profits. In this case, if the market does go up as high as you expect, you exercise your option to buy them at the lower price and then immediately turn around and sell them at market value or hang on for a bit longer and then sell them, depending on what your strategy is.

Chapter 3: How to Swing Trade

Getting started with swing trading is not too different from getting started with any other trading strategy when you look at the basic structure of this trading technique. Naturally, you need to find a stock that is going to offer you the best opportunity to increase your profitability, so you will want to look for a set of criteria to help you maximize your income. You will also need to validate that stock, and then execute your trade strategy, which is how you will actively enter, manage, and exit your position.

By now, you have a strong understanding of what your goal is with swing trading, so we are going to dig into actual strategies that you need to execute in order to effectively swing trade options. This includes how to swing trade with call options, picking the best positions, validating the position, entering and exiting trades, and knowing how to engage in risk management as you go.

How to Swing Trade With Call Options

When it comes to the options market, there are two types of options: call options and put options. Call options profit from the standard market philosophy of "buy low, sell high," whereas put options profit from the market that is decreasing. Put options tend to be more confusing to beginner traders, as they require a specific strategy in order for you to profit from a bearish market.

I want to give you an easy-to-understand and direct strategy for earning profit in a way that is going to be simple for you to follow, so we are going to focus on swing trading call options specifically. After all, the easier a strategy is to follow, the more likely you are going to profit off of it as you will not have to spend so much time studying it and remembering how to execute it.

There are two ways that you can enter a trade with a call option. One comes with writing and selling a call option, whereas the other comes with buying a call option. Writing and selling a call option should only be done on stocks that you already own and that are about to turn to a bearish direction as far as you understand. Holding onto stocks at declining prices means that you are going to lose out on value, so naturally, you would want to sell them. Alternatively, you want to buy call options on a bullish market when you anticipate that the value of those stocks will be increasing. This way, you can create profits from that rising value by purchasing the stocks at a lower price and then hanging onto them until they are worth enough for you to turn around and sell again.

Which situation you pick is going to depend on what position you are currently in with your portfolio. If you are new to trading, you likely have nothing to your name, which means that you are going to have to start with buying call options so that you can accumulate a portfolio.

However, once you have a healthy portfolio built up, you will want to start looking for opportunities to sell off your stock once it matures in value so that you can cash out on your profits. You will also need to continually buy new stock to make up for the stock that you are actively selling so that your portfolio remains full and healthy.

Picking the Right Trades to Enter

Getting started with buying call options for swing trading means that you need to pick the right trades to enter. The easiest way to do this is to start looking at assets that are due for a market correction. Generally, overbought and oversold assets are about to swing back into the opposite direction, which will start to give you a strong understanding of what positions might be available to you. This does not guarantee that they are going to be the best spots to trade *right now,* but it does indicate that there may be an opportunity for you to jump in on relatively quickly.

How to Find Support and Resistance

After you have found some possible locations for you to enter the market with, you are going to want to conduct some technical analysis to ensure that you have chosen the best positions possible.

The technical analysis that you are going to be conducting will ultimately help you find support or resistance in the trade, which will help you understand whether or not the position you are looking at is strong enough to earn you profits. Some positions you are looking at will have weak evidence surrounding them, suggesting that they are likely not ready to be traded yet.

Others, however, will have strong evidence proving that they are ready to be traded and that you can still earn a strong profit from them. These are the ones you are going to want to trade on.

Finding the support and analysis will require you to pay attention to the technical analysis that you perform, which will be complete with technical indicators that let you know how well a stock is performing. When you see "support" taking place in a stock, the stock itself is in a downtrend, and it is likely that the downtrend will temporarily pause due to a concentration of demand.

Alternatively, when you see "resistance" taking place in a stock, this means the stock itself is in an uptrend, but that uptrend is about to momentarily pause due to a concentration of supply. These slight shifts typically occur before the market is about to completely switch directions again, so seeing them indicates that the shift is about to occur.

They generally happen when the market has narrowed in on overbought or oversold but has not yet reached those particular points. Pay attention to these stocks as they will be switching fairly soon after this occurs.

When to Enter a Trade

With swing trading, your entry plays a massive role in your ability to earn profits from your stocks. With that being said, the entry itself cannot be refined to a science quite as clearly as exiting a trade since exits are always timed based on certain parameters being met.

While you can look for parameters with entry strategies, you cannot guarantee that what happens next in the market will be exactly what you anticipated it would be. As such, you will need to develop your skills in entering the market by looking for certain parameters and ultimately developing your intuition for what the best entry points look like.

Using the following guidelines will help you get a strong understanding of where you should enter the market, and then you can begin to develop your own intuition about when the best times are from there. With a combination of strategy and a good gut feeling, you can generally time your entry points with confidence.

Finding the exact parameters you are looking for when entering a trade will depend on what type of strategy you are executing. For example, if you are going to purchase a call option, you want to look for a market that is about to take a swing into a bullish market so that you are purchasing at the proper time. Alternatively, if you were to purchase a put option, you would want to look for a market that was about to swing into a bearish decline so that you were able to profit from that option.

In chapter 7, we are going to discuss multiple trading strategies you can use to earn money with swing trading options. As we discuss each strategy, we will also discuss exactly what to look for so that you can enter the market properly and start trading.

When to Exit a Trade

Exiting a trade is far more strategic and exact than entering a trade. Unlike with entering a trade, you can set exact parameters for when you can exit a trade, and the minute they are met, you can complete your exit. Regardless of what happens in the market after that point, you have already exited and have already met your goals, so there is no reason for you to continue following the market.

Anytime you plan a trade, you should always have your exit strategy planned before you ever enter the trade itself. Keeping your exit strategy clearly outlined ensures that you know exactly how you are going to complete the trade so that you can gain your profits. If you do not define an exit strategy beforehand, including a time and price point that you want to exit the trade by, you might find yourself sitting in a trade indefinitely with no clear outlines on how you are going to exit it. As a result, you might find yourself sitting too long and wasting time or losing out on profits because you did not exit at a reasonable time.

Just like with entering a trade, the exact strategy you organize around exiting a trade is going to depend on what strategy you used in executing the trade in the first place. For example, if you are buying a call option, you would want to exercise your contract when the market matures in a bullish position.

Alternatively, if you were buying a put option, when the market matures in a bearish position, you would want to exercise your contract. Exercising at the right time, based on the parameters you have set out for yourself, ensures that you are either gaining your intended profits *or* preventing losses on your investment. Which strategy you take will depend on whether or not the market actually behaved in the way you thought it would.

Where to Place Stop Losses (and Why You Need to)

When you are trading options, stop losses are a type of risk management tool that you can use to prevent yourself from enduring excessive losses to your trade value. With stop losses, your trading platform identifies a point at which you want to exit the market based on parameters you have set out and automatically removes you from the trade to avoid catastrophic losses.

With options trading, this tool is only used when you are selling options, as selling options can come with unlimited risk. When you sell an option, if the contract is overbought and you do not have enough stock to fulfill all of the contracts when they are bought, you would be required to purchase stock at market value and sell it.

This often means purchasing stock at market value and selling it for less than what it is worth, which means that you take a loss on every single share you sell. If you have to sell multiple shares to multiple contract holders, this can rapidly turn into a devastating loss. We are going to discuss other ways to prevent this from happening in future chapters, but in the meantime, know that a stop loss is one of the most basic and useful tools out there.

When setting a stop loss on an option, you are actually purchasing what is known as a stop *order*. This means that if the market goes out of favor of you selling your shares, for example, if you are selling call options and the market goes bullish instead of bearish; your stop order will automatically buy back all of the contracts you have out there. This means that you will no longer be engaged in any active trades, so you will not have to worry about having those trades existing, losing you massive amounts of money.

Setting your stop orders needs to be done properly as the market will naturally engage in a certain amount of volatility as the market moves forward. For example, the market itself might be moving in a bullish direction but takes a momentary bearish hit at a certain point before moving back into a bullish direction. If you were to set your stop orders ineffectively, they would sell, and you would still lose on your investment, even if the market continued into a positive direction after that momentary switch. With that being said, your stop order should likely be set a few clicks into the negative direction of any trade so that the market has room for movement.

This way, you might still incur a loss, but it will be managed by your stop orders, which means that you will not incur a massive loss. And, if the market swings back positive, no loss will be incurred at all, and you will continue to earn profits as expected from your trade, despite a normal amount of volatility taking place as the price reaches your preferred target value.

Chapter 4: Platforms and Tools for Options Trading

Every industry, no matter what industry it might be, requires certain platforms and tools to help them complete their jobs effectively. In the trading industry, this is no different. Traders require a certain type of platform and specific tools to help them execute their trades, as well as improve the quality of each trade so that they can earn more money from their investments. These platforms support everything, from actually moving money around and opening orders to completing the technical analysis, which is why they are so necessary.

When you get started in trading for yourself, you will also need to make sure that you have the proper tools to do this at a professional level. Being cheap about your platforms or tools can result in having inferior quality products that make it more challenging for you to engage in strong trades. In fact, they may even reduce the quality of your trades and impact your ability to earn a profit through swing trading options. Rather than shelling out a small amount of money now, realizing the quality of your platforms and tools are subpar, and then shelling out more later; it is better to start with the best. This way, you are not spending money twice when you only needed to spend it once. This is a great way to trade with a professional trader's mentality by minimizing your risk and maximizing your gains overall, even outside of actual trade deals themselves.

When you get started with swing trading options, you are going to need a brokerage, news platforms, and technical analysis software. All three of these will help you actually conduct and manage trades or perform adequate analysis of the market and the stocks you are looking at investing in to validate the quality of your trades.

Getting Started With Brokers

The rise of online trading has resulted in a massive number of online brokerages becoming available for traders to trade with. With that being said, there will be some brokers who are excellent and others that have significant drawbacks that may make them more difficult to trade on. As a beginner, these drawbacks can become even more challenging, so it is important that you steer clear of these particular brokerages and go with ones who are going to make trading easier for you.

Some experienced traders will advise brokerages that provide a bare-bones experience with very few additional elements available for traders to use. These are generally platforms that require you to have a fair amount of knowledge and understanding around what you are doing so that you can navigate these brokerage platforms effectively. Again, I recommend staying away from these for now because they may be too challenging for you to trade on early on. Later, you can always switch to a more basic platform if you feel that you would prefer it, but as a beginner, you should be looking for one that has all the right "bells and whistles" for you to get started with.

There are some fairly simple ways to spot a brokerage that is going to be best for you to trade on as a beginner. By paying attention to these criteria, you can ensure that you are working together with a brokerage that is both high quality and easy to navigate for a new trader. In particular, there are five important criteria you should look for when you are seeking out a brokerage to trade with.

Free Education Tools

With online brokerages growing in popularity, it is only natural that the brokerages are facing some serious competition in their industry. Some of these brokerages are going to attempt to set themselves apart by offering educational tools that you can use to help improve the quality of your trades, navigate their platform better, and ultimately earn greater profits. This is an excellent benefit to look out for among trading platforms because it proves that the brokerage knows what they are doing and that they are geared toward helping new traders get their foot in the door.

Some of the educational tools you might see on an online brokerage include educational and informative blogs, online options trading courses, webinars, one-on-one guidance, or even face-to-face meetings. All of these educational resources can enable you to improve your understanding of how their platform works, as well as how options trading works so that you can conduct better trades.

With that being said, it is important that you do not become complacent and rely exclusively on any given resource for your information. Even if that resource is the best source of information in the world and consistently shares high value and high-quality knowledge, you need to validate what you are learning through other platforms, too.

This is the best practice to get into as a trader, as it ensures that you never accidentally take on some bad advice or apply it in an ineffective way due to a misunderstanding. As a trader, it is always smart to ensure that everything you learn is truly the best possible information, as this is how you minimize your risk exposure, both inside and outside of the trading arena.

Excellent Customer Service

Working with a brokerage that is incapable of providing excellent customer service can be challenging, as you will not have access to adequate support if something goes wrong. It would be disappointing to have something on the platform not to work effectively or to be confused about how to navigate part of a platform, only to have no one to turn to for help. Even though online brokerages do require you to do your own trades, you should still have access to someone who can help you should anything go wrong. It is, after all, their platform that you are trading on, and it is the brokerage's responsibility to ensure that the platform works and that all of their consumers can easily navigate that platform.

Putting a brokerage's customer service to the test is fairly simple. First, you need to decide what type of contact you would prefer to have with your brokerage, ranging from chat, email, or phone support. Then, you need to take your preferred method of contact and attempt to contact the brokerage. In your communications, seek to get through with just some basic questions that will help you understand the platform more and get a better trading experience from it.

You can also directly ask what type of support is available to you should you need any help with your trades. A great brokerage will have excellent customer service that communicates quickly and answers every question that you might have. They should also make it simple for you to get back in touch with them if you have any further questions or concerns.

Easy User Interface

There are countless styles of platforms, each with different user interfaces. Some of them are basic and truly have no added bells and whistles, which means that you need to have a fairly complete understanding of what is required from you to conduct trades. Others are far more interactive and will essentially walk you through the process of making your trades. These ones also tend to make it easier for you to navigate their site and get access to whatever area or resource you need with ease.

Naturally, you want to look for a platform that is going to have an easy user interface. The last thing you need is to find yourself overwhelmed with a new style of trading and find yourself overwhelmed with a platform that is difficult to navigate. The easier the platform makes it, the easier it will be for you to place all your energy and focus on the trade rather than getting distracted by the platform itself.

Access to High-Quality Data and Tools

Every trader needs access to high-quality tools that are going to assist them with conducting technical analysis reports and identifying the best possible locations in the market. A strong brokerage platform will have an excellent range of data and tools that you can access to help you with those trades. As someone who is searching for a brokerage, it is your job to take a look to see what type of tools are available through the brokerage you are considering.

You want to pay attention to how many tools are available for you, what type of data is available to you, how relevant and useful these tools are, the quality of the tools, and the cost associated with these tools. Often, brokerages will offer a basic trading platform for the price of your license or membership, but they will require you to pay additional fees to gain access to their higher quality tools. You are going to want access to these higher quality tools.

Even if you plan on starting out as a basic trader, you should always look for a platform that offers the data and tools for you to grow into a more advanced trader. Looking into the long-term growth of your trading career will ensure that you are always planning one step ahead, which is a good rule of thumb for any trader to engage in.

Priced Within Your Budget

Before we get into discussions around the cost of the brokerage you are considering, we need to talk about a crucial mindset element of the cost associated with trading.

Many new traders will seek out brokerages and tools, often looking to pay the least amount possible. This is likely because they have no experience, so they want to "test the waters" before diving in full force, which is understandable. However, it can also be costly and is not a wise mindset to enter your trading career, no matter how passive or part-time you might want to be with your trades.

Picking a brokerage exclusively based on the cost associated with the brokerage itself can lead you to picking a subpar platform in exchange for a few bucks saved per month. As a result, you can find yourself struggling to execute high-quality trade deals because you are attempting to deal with the limitations of low quality or difficult-to-use brokerage.

The cost associated with a brokerage should *never* be a priority when you are choosing what brokerage you are going to use. Instead, see this as a high-quality investment that you are going to earn back quickly within your earliest trades.

With that being said, it is clear that different people are going to have different budgets around how much they can genuinely afford to pay for a brokerage. For that reason, you should certainly consider the costs and fees associated with the brokerage that you are looking to start with. Doing so will ensure that you pick one that is going to be priced within your range.

Another aspect of the cost that you want to consider is the cost of the brokerage versus the value you are actually gaining from that brokerage. Some brokerages will have enormous fees, yet they do not offer nearly as many services as other brokerages do, or they clearly have a platform with lower quality. Make sure that you pay attention to the cost versus the value to ensure that you are paying a reasonable cost to pay for the brokerage you are going to use.

Brokerages I Recommend Exploring

At the time of writing this book, there are three brokerages that I would recommend to any new trader as a possible platform to use. Remember, conduct your own research, and put these brokerages to the test by searching for the proper criteria on each one to ensure that you pick the best one yourself. Your confidence based on your own research should always be paramount in any decision you make.

TD Ameritrade

TD Ameritrade is easily one of the best overall trading platforms out there. This platform has excellent pricing, is easy for beginners to use, has access to great resources for traders of all experience levels, and has a top-of-the-line platform to execute your trades. It is easily the best platform for anyone who wants to increase the quality of their trades while also increasing their skills and earning maximum profits

Charles Schwab

Excellent for new traders specifically, Charles Schwab offers an extensive library of resources, low-cost commissions, and a wide range of tools to help you increase the quality of your trades. Charles Schwab also has excellent interfaces for any platform you might be trading on, from desktop to web or mobile, which means that you can easily take your trades on the go with you.

ETrade

For anyone looking to grow their skills, ETrade is a great platform to look into. This platform is the oldest online brokerage and is known for supporting traders at any level when it comes to an understanding of how trades work and increasing their skills in trading. ETrade offers access to great resources, learning tools, trading tools, and an easy platform for you to navigate.

Finding Reliable News Sources

A large part of trading involves you paying attention to what is going on in the news that may be affecting the stock market, the sector you are invested in, or the specific stocks that you have invested funds into. A rule of thumb in the trading industry is that if trading news hits mainstream media, it is already old news, and expert traders have already taken advantage of that news for their own gain. In other words, if you were not in on it before, you are not going to capitalize or protect yourself as effectively as those who had access to reliable news sources did.

In the trading industry, you need to pay attention to specific news platforms that make a point of accumulating information from the industry the *minute* it comes out. In other words, they post new news. These are the platforms you want to pay attention regularly to, as they will let you know what is going on in the market that will affect the stocks. Traders generally check in each morning, afternoon, and evening to see what is going on in the market so that they can make better trade deals. You should also use these as a part of your technical analysis research to see if there is any news available that either supports or opposes your possible trade position.

It is important that when you pick news sites to follow that you are picking ones that are reliable and known for offering high quality and relevant information. Picking a platform that tends to be behind or that republishes something that other higher quality platforms publish can result in you missing out on important information. As a result, you may still end up being late on the latest trends, which could reduce the quality of your trades.

Some of the best news platforms out there include Investors.com, Yahoo Earnings, Seeking Alpha, and CNBC. These platforms are known for having recent and relevant information regarding the stocks. Ideally, you should bookmark them in your browser for easy viewing and check in on them frequently to stay up to date on the latest stock information.

Technical Analysis Software

Technical analysis software is a high-quality form of software to invest in as a trader, but it is important that you use it properly. All too often, new traders will rely on technical analysis software as their exclusive method for completing the software, which can result in them getting into low-quality trade deals. While technical analysis software is certainly powerful and can improve the quality of your trades, it can also miss over important information, such as news articles resulting in it not always being the most accurate. Furthermore, you need to diversify your research and technical analysis strategies to ensure that you are protecting yourself and managing your risk.

Most technical analysis software are designed to take into account a variety of pieces of information about the market, including historical patterns and behaviors and current technical indicators to identify what is happening with the stock. Once it has taken all of this into account, it develops information about the probability of what is going to happen with that specific stock. In other words, it will tell you if the market is going to stay neutral or swing bullish or bearish, and it will generally tell you how much it is going to change, too.

The best way to incorporate technical analysis software into your own technical analysis is to use it to validate what you already anticipate or to help you identify if a certain position is worth looking further into. This way, you are using it to help you develop your case, but you are not relying on it exclusively. Although you could go either way, I recommend using a technical analysis software after you have already conducted your own technical analysis. This way, you do not do your research using confirmation bias, which essentially means that you are looking for information that validates the software rather than looking for information objectively.

There are multiple technical analysis software out there that you can try, although there are three that I recommend as go-to platforms for anyone to use. These three include Tradespoon, TradeTrakker, and Market Club. You can use 2-3 to validate your own research, as well as the results of the other software so that you can create a strong case for your trade and develop a high level of confidence in your next move.

- Tradespoon would be my personal number one recommendation as it has a strong algorithm that tends to produce highly accurate results. With Tradespoon, you can see the prices predicted into the future, and more often than not, it is on par or very close to what actually happens with those particular stocks. This is a great, reliable platform to use when conducting technical analysis.

- TradeTrakker is another great software that is simple and easy to use. This program will not only help you conduct technical analysis, but it will also help you manage and track your trades so that you can easily see what is going on with your open orders. This is a great multi-benefit tool to use as a trader.

- Market Club is a platform that has several different indicators available to be used on it. This particular software will provide charting, trading, and scanning resources, all of which are highly valuable for traders.

Chapter 5: Options Call and Put Orders

Engaging in trade in the world of options will require you not only to understand the difference between a call order and a put order but also when and why these two orders are beneficial. Creating a concise understanding of each of these orders will ensure that you are fully aware of what you are trading and how these tools are used to conduct strong trade deals.

To dig even deeper, we are going to further explore exactly what are the pros and cons of trading options so that you are fully aware of what you are going to experience when trading options. Fully educating yourself on the benefits and drawbacks of a financial instrument, such as options, enables you to get a clear awareness around what possible risks you may face in the market.

Understand that these risks can be gains from either the pros or the cons, depending on what they are. If you identify a pro regarding options only to become complacent in that area, for example realizing that options are less risky and behaving as if they have no risk, then this becomes a risk to your trades. For that reason, it is crucial that you understand both the pros and cons and recognize the weight of the risks that come with these trade deals. Doing so will help you hedge yourself against the potential risks so that you can trade more confidently and increase your profitability on trades.

Understanding Call Orders

Call orders are contracts that provide buyers the right to buy the underlying stock at the strike price, or predetermined price, outlined in the contract.

The individual buying the stock must do so before the contract expires; otherwise, the contract expires worthless, and they no longer have the right to buy the stock.

The individual responsible for selling the call order, also known as the "writer," is obligated to sell the stocks to the individual who purchased the call order should they decide to exercise their right to buy.

When a call order is written by the seller, they outline the strike price and expiry date. These two pieces of information tell the buyer how much they are buying the stocks and when they need to buy them if they are going to exercise their right to buy. Anyone who writes a call order needs to be willing to part with their stocks at the strike price by the expiry date as they are now obligated to sell their stocks at this price. This means that if they are missing out on profits or even incurring losses due to the price they have chosen, they still must uphold their obligation to sell should the buyer wish to exercise their right to buy.

Call options are bought by individuals in a long position and sold by individuals in a short position. In other words, someone who buys a call option and then buys the stock attached to the call option intends on holding onto that stock until the value of the stock increases. Alternatively, someone who sells a call option is in a short position as they plan on letting go of their stock within a fixed period of time. Generally, the seller only profits the amount of the premium paid for the contract and nothing more. The premium itself represents the cost paid by the buyer to acquire the contract, earning them the right to buy in the first place.

Understanding Put Orders

Put orders are the opposite of call orders as they give individuals the option to sell the underlying asset and give buyers the obligation to buy should the seller decide they want to exercise their contract. Put options are written by the buyers who agree to purchase stocks at a strike price by a certain date should the individual sell the stocks. Generally, swing traders who are trading options will alternate between writing call options and put options so that they can maximize their profits through options by leveraging either order type.

Put options tend to be the most confusing option variety for traders because of how they sound, but they are actually incredibly simple to understand and trade. The easiest way to explain a put option is to give you an example of what a trade involving a put option would look like so that you can see how they are organized and how profits are gained from these options.

Let's say you were going to invest in Intel, and the market value was $40 per share. Now, let's say you wanted to "protect" your gains in the market share prices. You would buy a put option at the strike price of $40 to enact this protection, which would give you the right to sell your shares at this price. This way, if the stock value drops, you are still able to sell it at $40 a share because the buyer is obligated to honor the contract. At this point, they would regain their values when the stock prices went back up, but they might experience quite a significant loss early on. Still, put option buyers—the ones writing the order—expect the prices to drop somewhat and are prepared to hold out the long position to earn their profits off of their investment.

Why Should You Trade Options?

If you want to take a short position and minimize your risks, trading options is an excellent way to lock into simple short positions that can earn you large profits over a fairly short period of time. By selling calls (for selling stocks) and selling puts (for buying stocks), you can take on several short positions to enable you to buy and sell your stocks rapidly, which will earn you quick profits.

In addition to enabling you to make quick profits, options actually protect your investments against the shifts in the marketplace. With options, you can lock in your right to buy or sell stock at predetermined values, enabling you to create a protection against shifts in the market. This way, if you think the market is going to drop, you reserve the right to sell your stocks at the higher price, or if you think the market is going to increase, you reserve the right to buy your stocks at a lower price.

In addition to structuring your trades this way, options have several other benefits and some drawbacks as well to consider. Take the time to read through them, and understand how they affect you as a trader so that you can keep yourself protected in the business of swing trading options.

The Benefits of Trading Options

When it comes to the benefits of options, it is always wise to see that each benefit is a possibility and not a given. In other words, not every trade is going to experience the same benefits, which means that you may experience some trades that result in not actually gaining these benefits. They are not guaranteed.

With that being said, there are several great benefits that come with trading options that are appealing to new and experienced traders alike. The most prominent of these benefits include cost efficiency, reduced risk, higher possible returns, and increased strategic alternatives.

Cost Efficiency

Options are considered to be a highly cost-efficient financial instrument because this strategy only requires you to purchase the *option* to buy, not the share itself. As a result, rather than paying out several thousands of dollars in stock, buyers can instead pay a significantly reduced premium for the contract offering them the right to buy the stock if they desire. For example, let's say a company has shares that are worth $20 each, and a trader wants to buy 300 shares of that stock. On the open market, this would cost the investor $6,000; however, they may be able to purchase three put options for $10 each, instead.

In this case, rather than shelling out $6,000 and exposing themselves to the risk that comes with a $6,000 investment, they have only shelled out $30 and exposed themselves to a possible $30 loss. Should the stock behave the way they anticipated it would; however, they can still buy the stocks for $6,000 even though the shares may already be worth well more than that. In this case, the buyer can exercise their right to buy, purchase the stock at the lower price, and then turn around and sell it at the current higher market value. Or, they might open a call order in which they will sell the shares, enabling them to possibly earn the value of the stock at the strike price, plus the premium paid for the order itself by the individual agreeing to engage in the trade with them.

Regardless of what strategy you use when you are in the trade, the cost efficiency alone with options is a wonderful benefit. Because you are not investing thousands or tens of thousands into the market, you are protecting yourself from any possible losses. The worst-case scenario will be that you lose out on the value of an option price, which reduces your loss to a few hundred or less, rather than a few thousand or more.

Reduced Risk

The exact scenario explained above with the lower costs and greater cost efficiency also contributes to options being reduced risk. Although they do not come with no risk, trading options exposes you to much smaller losses in most scenarios, as long as you set up your stop orders properly and execute your strategy according to plan. If you can stay on track and proceed with your trades, you can set yourself up for success and earn yourself a massive income from your trades in relatively minimal timing.

Higher Possible Returns

Because of how options trades are structured, you have the capacity to earn higher possible returns on your trades. The easiest way to understand this is to think of it this way: if you were to anticipate that the market was going to increase, but you were unsure as to whether or not you were right, you might wait to invest in the open market.

As a result, when the open market prices did increase, you would miss out on your perfect entry point and reduce your overall profits from the trade. If, however, you anticipated it to increase but weren't sure and you bought an option just in case, you would reserve the right to buy the stock at the perfect entry price, which would still afford you all of your profits.

By buying and trading options properly, you can hedge yourself against the right of being wrong while also increasing your possible profitability by locking in better ideal entry points. While there is still no way to perfectly calculate your entry point, you create a much greater opportunity to hold the best one possible based on your current knowledge.

Increased Strategic Alternatives

Options are known for being an incredibly flexible tool that can offer you the capacity to organize more strategic trade moves that may offer greater income per trade.

Traders who trade options are known for entering complex spreads that open several positions at once with the intention of maximizing possible profits off of each position while also minimizing possible losses off of each position. This way, they further hedge themselves while also increasing their capacity to earn a stronger profit. You will learn about some of these more complex spreads later in this very book, allowing you to earn the best profits possible, too.

The Drawbacks of Trading Options

As with any style of trading, there are certainly some drawbacks that you are going to need to consider. The biggest drawbacks with trading options include taxes, commissions, fluctuations in portfolio value, and uncertainty of gains. Each of these can impact your bottom line, so it is important to understand what they are and how they may affect the quality of your trades.

Taxed Gains

In the United States of America, all gains, including those earned from trading, are taxed as short-term capital gains. This means that they are taxed the same as your regular income in most cases, which can result in you paying high personal tax rates on your investments. In some situations, this may even boost you up a tax bracket which could result in paying a higher percentage in personal taxes for any given year.

It is important that if you get involved with options trading, you are aware of how much taxes you might have to pay and that you are setting the additional tax income aside so that you can cover it come tax season.

Commission Fees

Compared to other types of investing, options are known for having a higher commission fee per trade. Even if you are doing your trades on your own, you are likely going to have to pay a higher commission to your brokerage in order to be able to conduct your trades. This higher commission is gauged in comparison to the stock market itself, which tends to be significantly less pricey than options trading.

The best way to protect yourself from commission fees is to know exactly what you are going to have to pay for your brokerage. This means that you need to be aware of what you need to pay to maintain access to the platform, which typically comes in a monthly or annual fee and what you need to pay per trade. Most platforms will include both of these fee structures as a way to earn a profit from giving people, like you, access to their platforms.

Wider Fluctuations in Portfolio Value

Because of the way option trades are structured, there are bound to be higher fluctuations in your portfolio value. Because you are first trading in lower-cost investments and then possibly entering higher-cost investments, there can be massive fluctuations in the value of your portfolio. Furthermore, the options market is only open to certain stocks, and these stocks have a tendency to be volatile. This is a large reason for why they have stock options in the first place: to hedge people against the volatility of their stock values.

The best way to manage this risk is to make sure that you are fully prepared to handle the nerves and stress that can come with such massive volatility. We are going to discuss some powerful mindset tools later in this book to help you deal with this stress, which will significantly increase your capacity to stomach the changes.

As long as you continue to practice mindset strategies and hedge yourself against risks, this will be easier for you to handle. Even so, you may find this to be quite stressful and overwhelming in your trade deals.

Uncertainty of Gains

Lastly, options are generally built around an uncertainty as to whether or not a stock is actually going to behave in a certain manner, which is why options are preferred in the first place. Based on this uncertainty, there is always a higher level of risk that leads to many options expiring worthless rather than being traded on. Although the value of the option is significantly lower than the stock, which means the losses were far less than they could have been, there were still losses involved.

The best way to increase the quality of your trades is to use proper risk management tools and conduct thorough technical analysis on every trade you are planning on getting involved with. You can also exercise specific strategies on different trades that support you with minimizing your risk, ensuring that you are more likely to gain profits rather than encounter risks. Furthermore, a few great trades can offset the minimal losses on a few lower quality trades, meaning you are still likely to come out profitable in the end.

Chapter 6: Technical Analysis: Options Trading Opportunities

Technical analysis is your opportunity to identify and validate trades that you are considering partaking in. Through effective technical analysis, you can pinpoint exact locations in the market that are likely to earn you massive profits while also validating the quality of those locations for likely profitability.

It is crucial that you conduct thorough technical analysis for every single trade that you are considering partaking in. Not conducting thorough technical analysis could result in exposing yourself to massive risk unknowingly, resulting in you possibly taking on massive losses. With that being said, your goal with technical analysis is not only to identify and validate locations in the market but also to discover where possible risks exist so that you can protect yourself against those risks. While this will not completely eliminate those risks, it will help you minimize the impact that they could have on your trades.

Due to the thoroughness of the technical analysis, you are engaging in, you will also want to use this information to help you cultivate a trading strategy for the position you are planning on entering. This way, you can identify what spread you are planning on using, what risk management tools you are going to use, and what entry and exit parameters you are going to set for this particular trade. All of these points will be validated using your research, enabling you to feel confident that if you do choose to take on this position, you already have a clear understanding of how to leverage it to the best of your ability.

Conducting Fundamental Analysis

Fundamental analysis is a tool that traders use to identify the intrinsic value of a security based on relating economic and financial factors. Using fundamental analysis enables traders to understand what is taking place in the economy or in finances that will affect the position of a stock in the market. In addition to overall economic reports, fundamental analysis also takes into consideration the macroeconomics and microeconomics that may affect the company. Macroeconomics refers to the state of the economy and conditions affecting the industry as a whole, whereas microeconomics refers to things that affect a specific company, such as the quality of management running the company.

The goal with fundamental analysis is to identify a number that a trader can use to compare with a security's current price to determine whether the price is overvalued or undervalued. Depending on what they discover, this will influence their trading decision with that particular security.

Fundamental analysis is considered to be the opposite of technical analysis because it uses current economics and news to identify the direction of prices, whereas technical analysis uses historical market data to identify the direction of prices. Ideally, you should conduct both forms of analysis to see what results you end up with, as both should generally support the same theory you have. If they do, chances are, the stock you consider to investing in and the strategies you consider on using will be the best methods for you to move forward with.

Conducting fundamental analysis primarily requires you to identify current information that is directly affecting a company. This means that you are going to gather key information from any given company, such as their earnings press release, quarterly financial report, and annual financial report. You will then need to read the annual reports to discover as much information you can, regarding the company itself and where it rests in the market. Through combining all of this information, you can identify what is taking place in the company overall and what may be affecting the company right now.

As a swing trader, it is crucial that you understand both the long-term probabilities and the short-term probabilities so that you can generate a strong case as to whether or not it is a good idea to invest in this particular stock right now, even with options.

Gathering Key Information

The first step in fundamental analysis is gathering key information about the company so that you can get an idea of what is going on in the company. The key information you need to gather include the earnings press release, quarterly financial report (10-Q), annual financial report, income statement, balance sheet, and statement of cash flows. All of these reports are going to give you a strong understanding as to what is going on in the company and whether or not the current evaluation is above or below what it should be.

Earnings Press Release

The earnings press release that companies issue inform the public as to how their just-completed quarter in business went. This press release provides information around elements of the business, including revenue, expenses, and their gross profits so that investors can identify how well the company is performing and decide whether or not they want to invest.

The information in this report will also tell investors how to invest so that they are investing in companies in the best possible way. Earnings press releases are issued to investors in a press release first, and then they gradually leak into mainstream media headlines.

This is a great example as to why it is often stated that any news that is being shared by mainstream media is already old news.

Quarterly Financial Report (10-Q)

Shortly after the earnings press release is issued, companies provide the quarterly report, which is also known as the 10-Q report. This report provides finalized numbers based on what was already released in the earnings report. In many cases, the 10-Q report and the earnings press release look the same, but generally, the 10-Q will go into much deeper detail about the financial aspects of a business. It is a good idea to acquire this as soon as it has been released so that you can see how a company is performing in a more detailed manner.

Annual Financial Report (10-K)

The annual financial report is a complete document that you can receive for your fundamental analysis, making it an incredibly important piece of data to have. Annual reports detail full-year financial statements for the company, as well as any relevant developments that have taken place in the company that may affect their bottom line.

This document gives you a massive amount of information regarding how well a company is performing and what that company has to offer. Some companies will go even further and offer a version known as an annual report to shareholders, which contains even more detailed information that is specifically relevant to those who are invested in the company. If you can get your hands on this, get it. It will be helpful in analyzing the company itself.

Income Statement

The income statement is a simple document that lets you know how much a company is earning both in terms of revenue and in terms of how much profit it is keeping after paying all of their overhead. The income statement is important, as it lets you know how well a company is truly performing, rather than how well a company looks like it is performing.

Balance Sheet

Balance sheets act as a corporate version of a net worth statement for an individual. To put it simply, this document lets shareholders know what the company owes and what the company owns.

Statement of Cash Flows

Companies may have the capacity to report huge profits on their income statement, but this percentage is really not as impressive if you do not know how much cash is actually coming in the doors. The statement of cash flows shows you exactly how much money is coming in the door of the company and where they are allocating it to. The statement of cash flow also tends to show a more accurate reflection of what is happening in the company, as other reports can be distorted by accountants to create a better overall appearance than what is actually going on. With this report, you can get the cold hard truth and apply it toward your decision making.

Reading the Reports

After you have gathered all of the necessary information to conduct fundamental analysis, you need to know what to actually do with that information to understand what it all means. In general, there are six things you need to pay attention to in order to put this information together and generate a clear sense of where a company is at and whether or not they will be a strong company for you to invest in.

The things you need to look at include comparing reports, comparing cash flow to net income, evaluating operating and gross margins, looking for deterioration, the CEO's paycheck, and potential conflict of interest.

Compare This Year's Report to Last Year's Report

If you want to conduct strong fundamental analysis, you need to compare the current year's report to a report from the previous year. Conducting a side-by-side analysis lets you see whether or not the company is reaching the goals they have set for themselves and how well they are reaching those goals. If a company is not reaching its goals, you are going to need to continue your analysis to find out why they are not and how that is going to affect your investment.

Compare Cash Flow With Net Income

The easiest way to get a clear sense of how a company is doing is to compare their cash flow to its net income. Ideally, a company's cash flow should match up fairly closely with the amount that the company reports as profit. If you see any significant discrepancies here, it could indicate that the company is not performing well or that something shady is going on. In that case, it may not be a strong company for you to invest in.

Evaluate Operating and Gross Margins

Getting overly invested in the bottom line of a company is not a great way to make sure that you are gaining access to the best information possible. If you want to know how a company is performing, pay attention to its operating costs and gross margins. This helps you cross-reference the profits to ensure that the information being provided is accurate. Ideally, the company should be profiting somewhere close to the value of the gross margins.

Look for Deterioration

Before you invest in a company for its growth prospects, take a look to make sure that the company is actually growing. You do not want to invest in a company, assuming it will grow only to realize that it is deteriorating or losing value. A simple analysis of the company's fundamentals will give you an idea as to whether they are growing or not. If they are not, they may not be a strong company to invest in, as they may have hit a stalemate, or they may even be dropping in value.

Identify the CEO's Paycheck

As an investor, you want to make sure that the management of a company is concerned about its investors. If you are looking at the annual report and realize that the CEO or all of the top executives are being paid exorbitant salaries, it could mean that the management is more concerned with itself than anything else. This could mean that they make poor quality moves in terms of the stock value of their company in order to bank their own gains. As an investor, this is not a good sign.

Look for Potential Conflicts of Interest

Lastly, you need to look through the company's top-paid executives and see if there are any conflicts of interests that lie between them and their networks. Executives that are liaising with people or other companies who could pose a possible conflict of interest might be more interested in their own gains than the gains of their company. This could be a poor indicator of the outlook of investing in this company.

Conducting Technical Analysis

In addition to conducting fundamental analysis, you also want to make sure that you conduct a technical analysis to see how a company is performing in the stock market itself. While this is, in many ways, the opposite of what you are doing with fundamental analysis, it is still an important form of analysis. Technical analysis is done by looking at technical indicators and identifying the likelihood of stock moving in a positive direction for where you presently sit and the goals you presently have.

With technical analysis, you are not looking at reports of the company, but instead, you are looking at the company's behavior in the actual stock market, which will help you understand how it might behave going forward.

Ideally, your technical analysis should support your estimations based on your fundamental analysis so that you can feel confident in your trade. In other words, your technical analysis should show that the stock is about to partake in a specific pattern that makes logical sense to what you have already discovered through fundamental analysis. If you do not find this information to align, it may be a poor indicator for that particular stock at this time.

With technical analysis, you are specifically looking to identify direction, magnitude, and timing. You want to know what direction the stock is going to be moving in, how much it will move, and how long the move will take to occur. This can all be learned by reading the proper indicators and putting the information that you learn together to create a "case" for the stock you are researching.

Support and Resistance

The first thing you want to do is conduct price analysis and pattern analysis for the stock you are considering. You can do this by paying attention to the support and resistance lines that let you know whether a stock is successfully rising or declining at this time. Support and resistance lines, sometimes called zones, are lines that indicate where a stock has repeatedly reacted to higher (from support) or lower (from resistance.) price. In other words, if the stock is higher, it has been supported by those buying it, whereas, if it is lower, people have resisted buying it to the point where it has dropped significantly. You want to find a stock that has reached either a high point of support or a high point of resistance, as this indicates that it is likely going to change direction in the near future.

Moving Averages

The next thing you want to pay attention to on your chart, in addition to support and resistance, is moving averages. Moving averages tell you the general flow of the market and what to expect from the future flow. The moving average line rarely follows the exact pattern of the candlesticks themselves because it seeks to identify the general flow of the chart itself.

For example, if a chart is declining in value but experiences a small momentary increase in value, the moving average will not represent the volatility directly through hectic waves in its line. Instead, it will show the average decline is not quite as strong based on these subtle shifts in direction.

If a moving average line takes a sharp dive toward the bottom of your candlestick chart, you know that the price is crashing in that particular stock. Likewise, if it takes a sharp turn upward, the stock is likely gaining value quickly. The more common flow of the line, however, is large swooping waves back and forth that will help you identify what is going on in the market. By paying attention to the moving average over a set period of time, you can identify where the stock presently exists in its trading cycle and where it is likely to move next. For example, if the line generally rises and falls at the same rate and it is presently showing an uptrend, you should be able to gauge that the average is likely going to fall again fairly soon.

Indicators

The next part of conducting your technical analysis includes following indicators like the MACD, RSI, and stochastics indicators to see how the stock is performing and how it is likely to continue performing going forward. These indicators are helpful in understanding the strength and volatility of the stock, which can be helpful in determining what past patterns might indicate future patterns.

Reading each of these indicators can be done directly in your trading platform by looking at the current market charts and applying the appropriate indicators over those charts. If your trading platform does not offer these charts, you can also use a technical analysis software, such as one of the ones mentioned previously so that you can apply the indicators to the chart and begin reading its patterns effectively.

Moving Average Convergence Divergence (MACD) Indicator

The MACD indicator follows trends in the market, similar to how the moving average that we recently discussed does. Much in the same way, this particular indicator does not directly follow market movement in terms of volatility but instead takes the average of the volatility of the market and turns it into an indicator.

For the moving average convergence divergence indicator, you are actually following the moving averages of the highs and lows of the market. Typically, this technical indicator will be shown on a histogram rather than a current market graph so that you can see how the stock has behaved historically according to this indicator.

This indicator is shown by two lines: a blue line and a red line. Essentially, when the blue line (12-period EMA) is shown above the red line (26-period EMA), the market has a positive value, and when it is below, the market has a negative value. When they cross over, this indicates that a shift has occurred in the value of the market, moving it into either a positive or negative direction, depending on what direction it is coming from.

Relative Strength Index (RSI) Indicator

The RSI is an indicator that will tell you the magnitude of price changes in the market, ranging from overbought to oversold. The RSI will display on your chart as an oscillator, which means that it is a line graph that moves between two extremes to indicate the different directions of the market. This indicator carries a reading from 0 to 100, which indicates where the market currently rests and how likely it is to switch back into the opposite direction.

As a beginner, the easiest way to read the RSI is to identify where the overbought and oversold portions of the chart are. You will see this chart pop up below the active market chart in its own separate chart, but it will follow in the same real-time updates to show you what is actively going on at any given point. On that chart, there will be two frames, one at the bottom of it and one at the top. The bottom frame represents 0-30; the top frame represents

70-100. If the indicator is in the bottom frame, this indicates the market has been oversold. If it is in the middle of the frame, it is still in the process of moving from one extreme to the next. If the indicator is in the top frame, the market has been overbought in this particular stock. Anytime it reaches the overbought or oversold positions, the market is due for a shift back in the opposite direction.

Stochastic Indicator

The stochastic indicator looks very similar to the RSI, except that it features two lines instead of one. These two lines move very closely together, showing the strength of the market at both its highest strength points and lowest strength points. In a way, this chart reads somewhat like both the MACD and RSI indicators. With this chart, when the blue line is *below* the red line, the market is in positive value or bullish. When the blue line is *above* the red line, the market is in negative value or bearish.

In addition to the lines, this indicator also has two frames on the chart: one at the bottom and one at the top. The bottom frame is represented by the 0-20% portion of the chart, whereas the top frame is represented by the 80-100% portion of the chart. Ideally, you want to see *both* lines on the indicator cross into the oversold (0-20% frame) or overbought (80-100% frame) position to indicate that the entire market is about to shift. If only one line crosses into the frame, this means that a shift is likely to occur soon, but the market is not yet ready to completely shift in the opposite direction. This is not always the case, but more often than not, this is the type of patterns we see in stochastic indicators.

Using Past Results for Future Possibilities

With technical analysis, you want to use past results to indicate what is likely going to happen to the stock in the future. This works based on the theory that every single stock has a general pattern that it follows overall, assuming no significant news comes in and overrides the general pattern and that we can use this pattern to predict where the stock is going.

For example, if a stock has a history of crossing into overbought frames every 7 days and back into oversold frames every 7 days, we know that the average lifecycle of this stock is 7 days before it switches back into the opposite direction. Based on this, we can assume that the future behavior of this stock is likely to be fairly similar, possibly with a few days' difference per trade.

You accumulate your understanding of stock patterns by looking at the market itself and then applying technical indicators to actually read exact percentages and numbers around how the stock moves.

This is how you apply exact measures to the pattern so that you can not only visually pinpoint it but also recognize what prices and exact timelines are generally involved in each part of the pattern. By doing this, you give yourself a strong idea as to what is likely to happen again for this particular stock now, based on where it is in its current lifecycle and what you already know about the stock's historical behavior.

It is important that even if you have performed technical analysis on a certain stock in the past, you do it again every single time you are going to trade that stock. Even if you just finished a trade with it, and you want to enter a new position, you still need to complete your technical analysis again to ensure that you have done it properly. Attempting to skip the technical analysis at any point due to the belief that you already know what is going on and how to place yourself can expose you to massive risk. Every stock will experience subtle yet important shifts in its pattern over time. It is important that you pay attention to these patterns and that you always update your technical analysis to reflect these patterns as you go.

Putting All of Your Analysis Together

Now that you have completed both fundamental analysis and technical analysis, you can get a full scope on how your stock is likely to behave in the market so that you can make a confident trade in that stock. For options, specifically, the best way to develop your position is to identify companies that are likely to present you with strong positions based on fundamental analysis. You can generally find good companies first through news platforms and then validate and verify them through your analysis of the company itself.

After you have identified strong companies to invest in, you can use technical analysis to make sure that right now is a good time to invest in that company. If you find that they are not at the best point in their lifecycle for you to trade, you are going to want to wait until they are at a better point so that you can start trading then. This way, you are getting in on a strong stock when the market supports your profits with that particular stock.

Before you officially invest in the stock or options, make sure that you also pay attention to the latest news around the company to see how that company is performing right now. Any news coverage could indicate that an unexpected shift is going to happen to their prices, either with their prices rapidly switching into an overbought or oversold position. News as basic as information about an incoming change to the board of executives or the CEO or a rumor that was started about the company can impact trades around that company's stock, which may impact your investment. Naturally, this information will not become available through technical analysis, so you need to make sure that you are always keeping your eyes and your ears open for this.

Chapter 7: Understanding Chart Patterns and Trading Patterns

You already have a strong understanding of the fact that, as a swing trader, you want to capitalize on medium-term positions in the market based on significant shifts in prices that take place relatively quickly. Ideally, you want the shift to complete within a few days to a couple of weeks to ensure that you can profit from that shift without having to immediately jump into a new position, or hold your existing position for too long.

After you have already completed your fundamental analysis and technical analysis and have confirmed your position in the market, you want to go on to look for the best entry point for the stock that you consider investing in. This way, not only are you entering a strong stock, but you are also entering at exactly the right time. You can find these perfect entry points by looking for patterns that indicate when the stock is about to move into a positive trading direction. As an options trader, you want to look for these patterns and then buy your options when you see them so that you can lock in these entry positions without actually having to take on the stock just yet. Then, if the pattern plays out as you anticipated, and the stock price moves into your favor, you can go ahead and exercise your options.

There are five patterns that any swing trader should be looking for when it comes to identifying the best entry point. These patterns are called head and shoulders, cup and handle, triangles, golden cross, and death cross. Each pattern will indicate that the swing is about to happen, which means that you can go ahead and purchase your options. In some cases, the swing will not happen, or it will not happen as strong as you thought it would, which means that the position is not going to be profitable. In this case, due to having invested in options instead of the stocks itself, you have hedged yourself from a massive loss and are only out the cost of the option itself.

Pattern #1: Head and Shoulders

The head and shoulders pattern can be identified in a chart with a baseline and three peaks in the indicator that you are reading. The outside two peaks, or the first and third peak, should be about the same height, forming the "shoulders" of the pattern. The middle peak should be the tallest of the three, forming the "head" of the pattern. When you see this pattern, this predicts that a bullish-to-bearish reversal is going to take place in the trend. The three increases should all come back down to roughly the same baseline to indicate that they are indeed forming the head and shoulders formation with this pattern.

The head and shoulders pattern indicates that, after a long bullish trend, the market is about to experience a reversal. This pattern basically shows that the strength of the stock is starting to decline, but people are not quite yet ready to sell their shares. Instead, they are holding out for a better price so that they can top out their profits as much as possible. The third increase that takes place proves that the stock position is rapidly weakening as it fails to climb back as high as the "head" part of the formation, which means that it is finally ready to take its reversal. This is the best time to get into the market if you want to sell call options or buy put options.

The head and shoulders pattern does have an inversion pattern, which takes place at the bottom of the market chart. In this case, the exact formation appears except, this time, it is upside down with the shoulders reaching down toward roughly the same point, and the head reaches down even further. If you see the same formation taking place in an inverted manner at the bottom of the chart, it indicates that the same tug-of-war experience is happening in the oversold portion of the market. In this case, you can assume the market is about to turn bullish immediately after the second shoulder. This is the best time to buy call options or sell put options.

Pattern #2: Cup and Handle Pattern

The cup and handle pattern can be identified on any bar chart, such as a candlestick chart. This particular pattern is formed when the bars make a shape of a "U" and then have a slight downward drift immediately after. The "U" represents the cup, and the slight downward shift represents the handle in this particular pattern. The cup is considered to be a bullish continuation pattern, and it is often used to identify opportunities to buy call options or sell put options. Ideally, you should place your stop order slightly below the lower trend line for the handle to avoid incurring any losses while also maximizing your profits.

When the cup pattern takes place in the market, this means that the stock is testing old highs that were experienced previously from investors who were buying at that level. Generally, this pressure results in it taking a downtrend for a period before advancing higher again. Essentially, individuals trading in this stock are validating that the stock is going to perform as expected and not result in a terrible loss through trades. The center of the cup itself usually lasts anywhere from four days to four weeks, depending on the volatility of the stock and the strength of the stock itself.

In order to be a true cup and handle formation, the cup itself should not be too deep, and the handles should not be too deep, either. The handles should actually form toward the top half of the cup pattern, not falling below into the bottom half. This way, you can feel confident that the cup is designing a strong, positive formation for trading.

If the cup is misshapen or drops too deep, this indicates that the stock is volatile and that, while a bullish trend could occur, it is likely to be highly volatile and not as strong. You should focus on buying call options and selling put options when the cup formation occurs so that you can capitalize on the bullish market that is expected to follow.

The cup and handle pattern is another pattern that you want to trade through buying call options or selling put options to capitalize on the bullish market.

Pattern #3: Triangles Pattern

Triangle patterns are another form of continuation pattern that let you know when the market is ready to reverse so that you can start capitalizing from it using swing trades. There are three different types of triangles that you can look out for in triangle patterns, and each type of triangle could indicate that a shift is ready to occur so you will want to know what these triangles mean and how to read them.

These formations include the ascending triangle, the symmetrical triangle, and the descending triangle. Each one will indicate what direction the market is going and what you can do to capitalize on the market.

Ascending Triangle

An ascending triangle indicates that the chart is likely going bullish or that it is already bullish but that it is taking a volatile path toward the overbought position. This trend is easy to recognize but also offers a distinctive and fairly finite indication that you are at the perfect point to enter or exit your position, depending on what position you are currently in.

The ascending triangle can easily be identified with several small inclines and declines in stock value, with the declines dropping less and less every single time. If you were to draw a line under the decline points on the market, you would have a straight line (or fairly straight line) directly pointing toward the top of the market, indicating it was bullish and following the ascending triangle pattern.

Getting into a position like this offers you the opportunity to increase your capital in a volatile market; however, it can take a few tries to get into the position that is really going to earn you the best profits. The best way to time your entry into a market like this is to identify when the price has dropped to the point that is slightly above the previous drop, as this is likely where that triangle is going to bottom out. From there, you can enter by buying a call option or selling a put option. Then, you want to wait as the triangle pattern continues to increase. You are going to experience rapid increases and decreases in pricing, but it will likely end in profits, so long as you monitor the position. When the triangle continuation begins to slow down or stop, it is time to exit the position to ensure that you do not accidentally lose your gains due to holding the position too long. Also, if you see the continuation pattern beginning to stop you can identify this as being a point in the market where you can anticipate a reversal in the price occurring in the near future.

Symmetrical Triangle

Symmetrical challenges are a little more challenging to explain; however, they are still high-value patterns to follow, and they can give you a strong understanding of what you can expect with the market.

On your chart, a symmetrical triangle can be identified by seeing a market swinging back and forth in triangle peaks with the lows and highs equally drawing back toward the center with each shift. If you were to draw a triangle on your screen with the point on the right side of the chart and two lines ascending and descending at a perfectly symmetrical ratio, the peaks and drops of the pattern should follow those two symmetrical lines. When this happens, you have found a symmetrical triangle pattern.

The direction that will take place after a symmetrical triangle pattern is established largely depends on what direction the stock came into the triangle from. If it came in from a downtrend, it would exit with a downtrend after a few shifts back and forth. If it came in from an uptrend, it would exit with an uptrend after a few shifts back and forth.

The tug-of-war that takes place with the triangles is an effort by investors to get in on the rising stock value or jump out on the decreasing stock value so that they can maximize profits or minimize losses. This tug of war settles itself out after a few swings and then allows the market to head back toward the same direction it entered the pattern with. With this chart pattern, you can capitalize on the swings by getting in on one of the symmetrical ups or downs and then quickly selling on the next down or up position in the market, respectively.

Descending Triangle

The descending triangle pattern exists in almost the exact opposite manner that the ascending triangle exists. As you might expect, the descending triangle follows a continuation pattern in a bearish market where the stocks are heading toward an oversold market condition. In this instance, rather than following the trend of the lowest points of the volatile shifts back and forth, you are following the highest points of the volatile shifts back and forth. The peaks of the tallest triangles should all be generally descending in direction and in value, drawing a fairly straight pattern toward the bottom of the chart.

If you see a descending triangle pattern occurring, this is your opportunity to sell call options or buy put options to profit from the bearish direction of the market. With that being said, you still need to make sure that you watch the market closely to identify when the descending triangle continuation begins to slow down. When it slows down or stops, you know the reversal is due to come back around, and the market is likely going to swing bullish again soon. You will want to exit your position before that happens to avoid experiencing any losses from your investment.

With both ascending and descending triangles, it is important to understand that the reversals can happen rapidly, and it can be somewhat intimidating to follow. The frequent fluctuations in value swinging back and forth can be incredibly stressful, leaving you feeling as though you are at risk of losing everything, and fast. It is crucial that you practice strong emotional management and mindset skills when you trade triangle patterns to avoid letting stress dictate your moves and destroy the quality of your trade.

Pattern #4: Golden Cross Pattern

The golden cross is a pattern that can only be seen on a candlestick chart, and it provides a signal that indicates that the market is about to become bullish. This bullish pattern is generally a breakout from a bearish market, which means that a full bullish reversal is likely to come into play immediately following the cross.

You can spot the golden cross pattern by opening your market chart and applying the moving average technical indicator to the chart itself. You want to have one moving average line representing a 200-day moving average, and the other representing a 50-day moving average so that you can see the long-term and mid-term flow of the patterns on the chart. The golden cross itself will actually exist on the moving average lines, not the candlestick chart itself.

The golden cross can be identified by seeing the 200-day moving average line move straight or neutrally across the 50-day moving average line in a horizontal direction. Prior to the cross taking place, the 200-day moving average line should be above the 50-day moving average line, and following the cross, it should now be below it. The 50-day moving average line should be moving in a fairly steady upward trend to create the vertical line in the cross.

When you see the golden cross move into action on your chart, you know that the market is about to move to a more consistent uptrend, which means you can buy call options or sell put options to get involved in this swing trade.

Pattern #5: Death Cross Pattern

The death cross pattern is almost the exact opposite of the golden cross, with the pattern moving into a downward-facing cross that indicates the market is going to have a bearish breakout. This pattern is also seen on the candlestick chart using the moving average technical indicator. You will still need to use the 200-day moving average indicator and the 50-day moving average indicator for this particular pattern, so you can look for it on the same chart set up that you were looking for the golden cross on.

The death cross has proven to be one of the most reliable indicators of a bearish market breakout, with some of the most notable recessions taking place, following a death cross, including the major stock market crash of 2008. Investors who jumped out of the stock market at this point or those who bought put options and sold call options protected themselves from major losses following these crashes.

Not every death cross indicates a major crash in the stock market; however, it is always important to switch your position when you see these crosses to avoid a possible loss from resulting in catastrophic setbacks to your trades.

You will spot the death cross in the exact way that you spot the golden cross, except that the death cross will have the 50-day moving average falling into a strong bearish trend before crossing over the 200-day moving average. The 200-day moving average should still be moving fairly neutrally by crossing horizontally over the screen at the time of the cross taking place. Prior to the death cross being formed, the 50-day moving average should be above the 200-day moving average, and following the formation, it should have crossed over to below it. When this happens, forming a cross pattern at the point where they intersect, you know it has moved into a death cross position.

Chapter 8: Mindset: How to Control Your Emotions Like A Pro

Many new traders believe that the biggest part of getting involved in trading is knowing how to conduct trades themselves, but this is actually not true. While knowing how to trade using the right platforms properly is crucial to making trade deals and making smart trade deals, it is not the only most important part of trading. A second and equally important part of trading has nothing to do with trading at all and everything to do with you and your ability to manage your emotions and stress.

If you want to become a pro trader and earn massive profits from your trades, you are going to need to be able to stomach the stress that comes with trading. Stress can enter in all different ways when you are trading, such as by watching the volatility of stocks and fearing that your plan is not going to play out as you assumed it would. If you allow stress and fear, among other emotions, to become excessive, you are going to have a hard time trading. You will find that you consistently make illogical moves in favor of your emotions, resulting in not being able to complete your trades in favor of your profits.

Effective trading strongly requires that traders be able to trade objectively to avoid being overruled by their emotions. This way, they can wait out the volatility of the market and earn strong profits as a result. Being able to trade objectively also means that you will be able to manage your losses by exiting trades when a loss has been experienced, rather than attempting to pivot your strategy and hold a longer position, possibly resulting in greater losses.

When you learn to trade, you should focus on managing your emotions, both inside and outside of trade deals. Managing your emotions and stress at all times will ensure that you do not let external stress or emotions affect your trading decisions, enabling you to make better quality trades.

Using Plans to Manage Emotions

Throughout this book, you may have noticed that I have frequently expressed the importance of formulating a clear strategy, including an entry, management, and exit plan *before* you begin any trade. Creating plans is an excellent way to make sure that you have effectively planned for any possible risks to be managed, enabling you to perform better in your trades.

Creating plans is not only effective for helping you with risk management; however, it is also effective for helping you with emotional and stress management. When you know what to expect, and you are aware of what is supposed to happen, it is easier for you to cut out any feelings of uncertainty when it comes to trading. Cutting out uncertainty with your trades means that you are more likely to feel confident in each step, making it easier for you to justify your logical reasoning and do away with your desire to act on stress or fear. In the end, this is going to make it far easier for you to manage your emotions and stay on track with positive trade moves.

You should have a few different cornerstone plans in place for your trade deals so that you always know what to expect, and you are always able to navigate situations logically and purposefully. Your plans should include planning out your day, your trades, and what you will do to manage your emotions. With all of this in play, you will be ready to make strong trade deals every single time, without the fear of emotions coming in and destroying the quality of your trades and your bottom line.

Creating a plan for your day can easily be done by deciding how you are going to execute your trading day. You can also incorporate a specific time for stress management so that you are not bringing stress with you into your everyday routine. A great example of a plan for your trading day includes starting out by researching the general market, identifying possible trade positions, checking in on your existing trades, taking on new positions, managing them, and exiting trades that are matured.

Your actual trade plan can be created when you have identified a new position to take on and have decided to carve out a plan for how you are going to trade that position. This includes understanding what type of strategy is likely going to work best for you, what entry and exit points are going to be best, and when you should call off the trade if losses start to creep in. This way, you are always prepared for exactly what needs to happen with every single trade deal.

With your emotions, it is important to have a plan for how you are going to manage emotions if you find that large amounts of fear or uncertainty begin to set in. Having a plan already in place for when you feel these emotions ensures that you handle them logically every single time, rather than attempting to construct a plan to release your emotions that are influenced by the active emotion you are experiencing. Something as simple as a logical check-in with facts and the way things are really going can be incredibly helpful in creating your plan to manage emotions.

Cutting Out the Unnecessary Stuff

As a beginner, you might find yourself struggling to discern the difference between trade practices that are necessary and trade practices that are not necessary. You might also find yourself taking necessary trade practices and unnecessarily making them more complex or time-consuming than they need to be. A great way to make better trades and manage your emotions more effectively while trading comes from cutting out all of the unnecessary stuff and just sticking to the bare basics of trading. The more straightforward and simple you can keep everything, the less likely you are going to trigger the interference of your emotions with your trade.

For example, let's say you enter a new open trade, and you have a plan already prepared for how you are going to manage that trade and exit it when the time comes. Maybe you have decided that at certain points each day, you will check in on that trade and any news affecting that trade to ensure that you are still holding a strong position.

These are all positive, necessary things to do in order to execute a strong trade deal. However, let's say that rather than periodically checking in, you start obsessively checking in. Maybe you noticed a headline that may affect your trade deal, and now you are obsessing over every single news platform and refreshing the page as often as possible to try and get any new information as soon as it comes out.

While it is important to get that new information, obsessing only makes you more stressed out. Each time you refresh, and there isn't any new news available, your stress levels increase more and more, leaving you wondering when more information will be made available and when you will be able to find out exactly what is going on.

Realistically, all of the additional check-ins in the aforementioned example are unnecessary and are simply creating more stress, not creating more factual evidence to influence a trade decision. Instead of creating this unnecessary stress, you could choose to check in again a few extra times that day and then set the boundary that you will remove yourself from the website after you identify any new information, should it be available. If you do not see any new information, set the boundary that you will leave it alone and wait until your next scheduled check-in.

By keeping everything simple and sticking to logical and straightforward plans for how you will conduct your trades, you can feel confident that you are going to make stronger trades. This way, you are no longer stressing yourself out with unnecessary information and extra steps. Instead, you are keeping it simple. As a result, your emotions easily stay removed from the situation, enabling you to move forward confidently and objectively.

Removing Negative People

Many people are fairly negative about trading, especially those who are completely unaware of how it actually works. Especially after the memorable stock crash of 2008, many have accumulated unreasonable beliefs that the stock market is a very dangerous place and that anyone who trades is guaranteed to lose money. To a degree, that is true. You are guaranteed to lose money—every trader loses money. When you make an investment, and it doesn't go as planned, you lose money.

However, you are unlikely to lose the massive amount of money that many people seem to believe that everyone is guaranteed to lose should they get involved with trading. In fact, as long as you trade right and pay close attention to the market itself, you are likely to always stay earning more than you are losing, which means that you are still coming out profitable with your investments.

Keeping negative people in your circle who are only going to feed you negative information or misinformation about the stock market will likely result in you feeling negative about it yourself. As soon as you begin to accumulate feelings of doubt and uncertainty, your chances of becoming successful in the stock market begin to dwindle drastically. You will be so afraid of experiencing those catastrophic losses that uneducated and negative people have filled your head with that you will have a hard time trading clearly and confidently.

Focusing on Just One Thing

It is a proven fact that people cannot effectively multitask and that, by doing so, we both reduce the quality of the tasks we are attempting to complete and increase the amount of stress that we experience at the same time. Naturally, neither of these is a good experience for you to have when you are attempting to earn an income by trading in the stock market, even if you are trading the typically safer alternative of options over stocks.

Creating a strong focus around each task you are engaging in will ensure that you are not amplifying your stress by overstretching yourself and that you are completing every task to the best of your ability. Furthermore, doing just one thing at a time will support you with fully understanding how each step works and how you can maximize it for higher profits and lower losses, especially as a beginner.

For some people, staying focused is challenging, and you might find yourself flitting your focus back and forth naturally. If this is the case, teaching yourself to stay focused will help. You should seek to practice this in all areas of your life, so you are not carrying bad habits from other areas of your life into your trading practices.

Setting Strong Goals

Goals are a wonderful tool that can help you increase your focus while also giving you a clear sense of direction for where you want to go with every trade deal you plan on making. When you set strong goals for yourself,you increase your sense of purpose in each trade you make, which means that you are more likely to create strategies that will earn you profits. Furthermore, you will have a meaningful reason for why you are trading in the first place, which will give you a greater desire to actually turn each trade into something successful.

When you set goals for yourself in trading, you should get as personal as you can so that your trade goals actually mean something to you. This way, you are more likely to stay focused, and you increase your ability to actually turn those goals into something. Your goal can be anything you wish for it to be, with popular goals ranging from things like wanting to retire with more money to wanting to travel the world with your profits. As long as it is something that drives you, it is a strong enough goal to keep you focused and successful in trading.

Another form of goal you can use in trading is known as "micro-goals," and they are used to set short-term goals for what you are seeking to accomplish in the immediate future. These goals are typically designed to help draw you closer to achieve your overall trading goal by serving as milestones that prove you are moving in the right direction. You can set micro-goals around how you want each specific trade to perform and what your purpose of that trade is, as well as by setting goals for monthly or quarterly earning goals. This way, you have a practical means for measuring your success with trading.

Managing General Stress Levels

Apart from managing stress and emotions within your actual trades, you also need to ensure that you are managing your stress levels in general. It can be surprisingly easy to experience stress in one area of your life and draw it out into other areas of your life, no matter how emotionally intelligent you might be. Even people with the strongest ability to compartmentalize and approach each area of their life with a fresh perspective can experience stress pouring into various areas of their lives due to a high amount of stress in any given area of their life. By managing your stress levels in general, you can significantly reduce the stress that you are carrying over into your trades that is affecting your ability to focus on trades by proxy.

There are many ways to manage your general stress levels, although the most simple and effective ones come from focusing on taking better care of yourself overall. By getting adequate rest every night, fueling your body with nourishing food, and exercising on a regular basis, you can take care of yourself in a way that makes you more resilient toward stress.

You should also take measures to manage added stress when it comes, such as by talking to someone or keeping journals that allow you to vent about how you are feeling. These things may seem completely irrelevant to your ability to trade, but you would likely be surprised at how much better you trade when you are not carrying any stress into the market from other areas of your life.

No amount of stress management is too much when it comes to trading, as it helps you trade better.

Starting Easy and Increasing Stress Tolerance

As a new trader, it can be easy to feel the pressure to attempt to recreate what other experienced traders are already doing on a regular basis. You may jump into the market assuming that you need to have several open orders right from day one and that you need to be managing all of these trades consistently over time in order to create a stronger bottom line for yourself.

The reality is that these are all experienced traders who have likely spent plenty of time increasing their skills and improving their stress management over the years. They also likely started out much easier and then increased the number of trades they took on over time until they reached the point where they are today.

What I am saying is this. Attempting to jump immediately to the level of an experienced trader before you have even given yourself enough time to understand how trading works is nonsensical. It will almost certainly lead to losses, possibly even the catastrophic ones that your overly concerned friends and family were trying to warn you about. It will absolutely lead to you being incredibly stressed and likely mismanaging trades due to being overwhelmed and having no idea as to what you are doing.

A better way to increase your skill while also managing your stress is to start easy and increase the difficulty of your trades and the number of trades you are engaged in, over time. By taking it slow and performing intentionally, you can feel confident that you are not at risk of overwhelming yourself to the point of not being able to effectively manage your trades.

Another benefit to starting easy and gradually increasing your skill level is that this will enable you to build your stress tolerance, as well. You will find that the more gradually you increase your skills, the easier it is for you to manage stress because you become an expert at managing each increasing level of stress. Over time, you will be managing massive amounts of stress-inducing trades like a pro because you will have taught yourself how to manage them properly. At this point, you will be trading like an expert, and it will happen much faster than you think, as long as you start smart.

Checking Yourself and Your Intentions

Finally, it is important that you always check yourself and your intentions before you make any decision in the market, even if you think that decision is calculated and logical. It can be easy to experience fear and attempt to make a logical plan for how you are going to manage that fearful position, and then genuinely believe that you are behaving logically because of the way that fear plays in our minds.

However, if you are structuring plans out of fear, there is a strong chance that the plans you are forming are not entirely based on logic and objection. This is why it is so important to make your plans and organize your entry and exit points, as well as your management strategies before you enter a trade. Before a trade, your entire plan is theoretical, and there is no money involved, yet it is so easy to think objectively and logically about that trade.

However, once you enter the trade, money becomes involved, and stress begins to increase. At this point, any alterations you attempt to make to your plan could very well be rooted in fear rather than logic and could completely negate the plan you set into place beforehand.

This is the biggest reason that you are always supposed to stick to the original plan rather than trying to change the plan partway through.

Checking in with yourself to see what your intentions are and what has inspired your current decisions will help you feel confident that you are making decisions from a place of logic and reasoning and not from a place of emotion. If you are inspired to take action due to emotions, it is imperative that you observe them objectively and logically as much as possible to really understand whether or not this decision is a good one. Not every decision rooted in emotions is a bad one, but most will be, so play it cautious, and always rely on logic and reasoning over emotions.

Chapter 9: Risk Management Strategies and Diversification

Whenever you are engaging something that involves your money, especially in a way that is not guaranteed, it is crucial to engage in risk management strategies that will prevent you from exposing yourself to more risk than necessary. With risk management strategies, you can feel confident that you are more likely to profit and less likely to lose, therefore making your trade deals stronger.

Investing in trade deals require you to consider four important areas of risk management to ensure that you are fully protecting yourself as much as possible. While this will not guarantee that you will not experience any losses, this will support you in minimizing the likelihood of experiencing excessive or massive losses. These four areas of risk management include basic money management, hedging with options, leveraging your mindset, and controlling your addictions and obsessions.

Basic Money Management and Diversification

The first thing you must do in order to protect yourself against risk is learning how to manage your money properly, especially when it comes to trading and investing. The way you manage your money with trades will be quite different from how you manage your money with anything else, and it is important that you learn the differences and apply them from day one. This way, you are not managing your money irresponsibly and exposing yourself to far too much risk.

There are four significant ways that you need to manage your money when it comes to trading: never investing too much into one trade, diversifying your trades, always keeping enough to complete the trade, and cashing out on a regular basis.

In trading, it is generally advised that you do not invest more than 2-5% of your total trading capital into any single trade so that you are not going all-in on any one stock. This rule is simple and follows the concept of "don't put all your eggs in one basket." If you have too much invested in one trade, and that trade goes sour, you are going to be out of a lot of money.

Ensuring that you never invest too much in one stock directly supports you in properly diversifying your trades. By investing in multiple investments at once, you ensure that any losses you experience are offset by the profits you experience in other trades. The idea here is that the profits you gain will be plenty to offset the losses you experience so that, despite losses, you are more likely to earn significant profits over time.

As an options trader, you also need to make sure that you keep enough money on hand to exercise a buy option should you decide to. This way, if you are engaged in an order that is going to afford you the opportunity to buy the stocks you want, and the market goes in favor, you have the cash required to actually buy those stocks at the strike price. If you spend all of your money on options and you do not have the funds to exercise an option, you have pretty much given up your ability to earn a profit from them, which means you have wasted your time and money.

Finally, part of risk management is knowing when to cash out. While you do need to keep your brokerage account filled with money to trade with, keeping it overflowing is not ideal. Having too much money in your brokerage account can lead to exposing yourself to risk if anything happens to the system itself.

While it is rare or highly unlikely that anything happens, it is not something you want to expose yourself to with your funds. Ideally, you should only keep what you plan on trading, and everything else should be cashed out. With that being said, the amount that you invest in trades should grow as you earn more, so you can expect that the cash value in your brokerage account will increase over time.

Hedging Risk With Options

Swing trading with options is one form of risk management in and of itself, for all of the reasons that you have read right here in this very book. From reducing the amount of capital that you have tied up in each investment to provide you with the opportunity to trade on positive swings and pass up on negative swings, there are many benefits that come with trading options.

Many expert traders will continue to use options to hedge their trades, particularly if they think those trades are going to be riskier, or they plan on trading a higher volume of trades because they can help you minimize the losses. While losses would still be experienced if the market did not mature the way the trader anticipated, they would not be as significant as they may have been, had the trader went all-in on open stocks.

If the trade does go as the trader anticipated, then they will have reserved the position to get in on the trade that would maximize their profits, enabling them to take advantage of that trade, retrospectively. Naturally, this can lead to rapid profits that will result in the trader maximizing their productivity on the market and increasing their overall income from trading.

Leveraging Your Mindset

Your mindset cannot be overlooked as being one of the most important risk management tools that you can use to help you minimize your exposure to the market. If you are always leveraging your mindset properly, you can increase your ability to hedge yourself against risks and prevent unnecessary losses on the market.

The best way to leverage your mindset is to start applying all the emotional management tools we discussed in the previous chapter. You can also begin working toward keeping yourself open and curious about the market so that you are always willing to learn and grow. If you are always interested in discovering more about how things work and how you can improve your skills, you will always keep yourself open to making better trade deals, which will result in earning higher profits.

Finally, make sure that you stay humble in the market. Never let yourself move into arrogance or the unwavering belief that you cannot lose because you can. If you develop this level of arrogance, you will almost certainly lose out on your profits and create massive exposure in the market. Stay humble, always complete every step of the trading tasks, and always recognize that you are exposed to risk no matter what, strictly based on the fact that you are invested in the market in the first place.

Controlling Addictions and Obsessions

In trading, it can be easy to become addicted to or obsessed with certain things that you believe make your trading fail-proof, which can, in turn, result in exposing yourself to higher levels of stress and risk. For example, in the last chapter, I pointed out how developing stress or fear and then constantly refreshing your page for more information about a stock can be a dangerous game to play, as it can expose you to massive risk through emotional interference. This is not the only way that your addiction or obsession can affect you in the market, however.

Anytime you notice yourself experiencing an addiction to or obsession with anything, ranging from a specific tool to a certain news source, it is crucial that you step back and make yourself objective once again. Obsessing over any specific tool, such as a certain technical indicator or specific technical analysis software, can result in you relying far too heavily on that tool. As a result, you may find yourself no longer trusting in your own experience and beliefs around the market and exposing yourself to massive risks.

Always make sure that you are diversifying not only the investments you make but also the tools you use to help you make those investments. Be willing to learn about new technical indicators, new companies, and new strategies, and practice applying them to your trades. Not only will this increase your skills, but it will also help you improve your flexibility and stay more calm and confident in your trades.

Chapter 10: An Example of a Trade

You have come a long way in understanding swing trading options, to the point where you should now be able to conduct a successful trade confidently and earn a profit from it. With that being said, you want to make sure that you are not accidentally picking up any fluff or any extra tasks that are unnecessary to trading due to not having a clear, bare-bones structure for how each trade should be completed. As you know, removing unnecessary steps in trading will help you stay more focused, will support you with managing your emotions, and will reduce your exposure to risk.

Below, you will find a simple-to-follow bare-bones structure of a trade so that you know exactly what you need to do, and you can cut out everything else. I suggest keeping this chapter handy and reflecting on it every time you are going to engage in a trade so that you can feel confident that your trade has been completed properly. By following it exactly, you will ensure that you have done everything you need to do to conduct a successful trade, nothing more and nothing less.

Create a Watchlist

The very first step in conducting any trade is creating a watchlist. A watchlist is a list that you compile of possible trade moves that you could make that are likely to earn you profits. Your watchlist is not a list of guaranteed positions that you have already analyzed and validated as being the best position. Instead, it is a list that highlights positions that are likely to be validated as positive trade positions that are going to earn you profits from your investments.

You can compile your watchlist by first looking at news sources to see what stocks are performing well and what stocks are not. Naturally, you want to keep any high-performing stocks on your radar and steer clear of the ones that are obviously not doing so well. Any stocks that are not in the news may also be positive to trade since nothing significant is going on with them, so if you have preferred stocks that you like trading, you can always add those to your list at this point, too.

Next, you want to go to your trading software and look at each stock in the market. For now, just take a look to see how it is doing. If it is performing well, add it to your watchlist. If you realize it is not performing so well or not moving favorably for a strong swing trade, you should remove it from your watchlist, as this will not be a stock you want to invest in. At this point, you want to minimize your list to roughly 2-5 positions that are likely to be the best ones, depending on how many trades you want to open.

Identify the Best Position

With your 2-5 ideal stocks in mind, you want to identify the best position for you to take for your current trade. If you are conducting multiple trades at one time, you should complete from this part of the trade forward for each individual stock you are looking at so that each investment is the best one.

This is the point where you are going to do your technical analysis. Here, you are going to put all of your efforts into validating the quality of the trades so that you can see which ones are likely to perform the best. Even though they may all perform positively, you want to pick the ones that are most likely to perform the best.

As you perform technical analysis on each stock, make sure that you are also formulating a strategy for how you would trade that specific stock. This is the point where you can make sure that your strategy fits what is actually going on with the stock, and since you are exclusively focused on analyzing that one stock at that moment, you will be most likely to construct a strong plan. Even if it does not end up being the trade you will make, you should have a complete plan in place in case it is.

After you have successfully technically analyzed all of your chosen stocks, it should become fairly obvious which stock is going to be the best for you to invest in. Ideally, it should be a stock that is most likely to earn profits with the least amount of risk possible. When you identify that specific stock, you know you have found the right one for your trading needs.

Time Your Entry

With your stock now chosen, your next step is to time your entry. This is where you want to pay attention to the patterns we talked about in chapter 7 to ensure that you are timing your entry properly. When you are starting out, you can keep this book handy and keep chapter 7 open when you are preparing to time your entry. This way, you can directly identify any possible patterns that may indicate that you have arrived at the best possible time for you to enter into a trade deal.

As soon as you see the patterns turn favorable for you to enter the market, you want to go ahead and open your option order. Make sure that you enter the order at the strike price and expiry date that you defined as the most favorable during the planning stages so that you are getting into the contract that is going to give you the best profits. Buying into a contract that has a different strike price or the wrong expiry date can result in not being able to leverage the position as strongly as you planned on it, possibly exposing yourself to more risk. Make sure that you invest properly.

Manage Your Position

After you have entered your trade, the next part is fairly simple. At this point, you are going to manage your position by periodically checking in on your deal and making sure that it is performing as you hoped it would. Ideally, your trade deal should be going according to plan, and your chosen stock should be moving in a positive direction. If it is, you can continue to check in every so often to ensure that this continues.

Your goal with managing your position is to make sure that you time your exit perfectly. You want to be looking out for any indicators that the market is about to reach your targeted profit or that it is moving in the wrong direction, and you are being exposed to more risk. The moment it moves into position to reach your targeted profits or a position that indicates you have reached your maximum risk tolerance, you want to be ready to exit the market.

With options trading, this part is not so challenging. While you do need to be ready to exercise your option at the right time when the market goes in favor, in most cases, there is nothing you need to do if the market goes out of favor. The only time that you would want to act is if the option you are selling has moved to the point where you are now at risk of having to pay a huge loss to fulfill the contracts you have entered. In this case, you want to close the order by buying back your contracts.

Exit Your Position

As soon as the market reaches your desired position, you need to be ready to exit that position. If you exit too early or too late, you run the risk of losing or missing out on profit, so make sure that you time your exit exactly accordingly to your strategy that you laid out during technical analysis.

When you exit your position, it will be because of one of these three reasons: you are losing money, you are not gaining money, or you are in a profitable area.

If you are losing money, you want to exit your position at your maximum loss tolerance point as outlined in your plan before going into the trade. This way, you can feel confident that you are not going to lose any more than you anticipated you would should the deal turn sour. In options, the only time this happens is if you are in a position where you are obligated to sell a stock, and it looks as though you are going to have to sell and take a huge loss. If you can, you want to buy back the contracts to minimize your loss.

Not gaining money differs from not losing money in that the position you have entered is not making a big enough shift to earn you enough profits to make a move worth it. Or, it may even move in a position where you would lose out if you were to exercise the contract. This happens most often when people are in the position where they have the option to buy, and the stocks have tanked, resulting in having the option to buy a bad stock. Naturally, they do not want to, so then the stock would expire without worth.

Lastly, if you are in a position where your option went as planned, and you are profiting from it, you would want to exercise your option. In this case, you close out at a pre-determined point, and you earn your profits from your trade. Exiting due to the market turning in favor may happen on or before the expiry date of an option, depending on whether or not the turn happened on or before the expiry date.

Review Your Process

Anytime you exit a trade, you should always be prepared to review your process to ensure that you have done your best in that trade and that you are clearly aware of any areas that you can improve your trade skills. This is an important area of opportunity as this affords you the ability to clearly understand what you might have done better to improve your profits or to avoid a loss that you may have experienced.

Chapter 11: Tips for Becoming an Expert Trader

The goal of any trader is always to educate themselves on how they can become a better trader. As a trader, you want to make sure that you move beyond basic beginner levels of experience and into levels that are more likely to secure you larger profits while also helping you feel more confident in your trades. Becoming an expert is based on your own experience and accumulating your own book of trade secrets based on trades you have actually made. However, it is also learning how to follow expert advice and applying it in a way that helps you feel completely confident in what you are doing.

In this chapter, I am going to help you identify the top six strategies that are going to take you from being a beginner to being an expert as quickly as you can build confidence in them and in yourself. These tips include consistent research, keeping a journal, validating your plans, learning from others, cashing out, and taking breaks to have fun. All of these tips may seem small or even irrelevant to you right now, but you are about to discover just how important and valuable these tips truly are. I suggest you start applying them to your trading style right away so that you can move from beginner to trader much faster.

Consistent Research

One way that experienced traders manage to increase their skill level and become expert traders is through consistently engaging in informative research. Experienced traders never assume that they know everything, even if they have been successfully trading stocks for years. They know that patterns are always changing, the market is always evolving, and there is no way that they could ever know everything that there is to know about trading on the stock market.

Rather than becoming complacent and exposing themselves to an increasing level of risk in their trades, expert traders constantly do research and do everything they can to learn more. They read books, follow blogs, pay attention to news articles, attend seminars, and network with other traders to increase their skills. If anything becomes available for them to increase their knowledge in the market or improve their results with certain strategies, they will take advantage of that to see if they can apply it to produce better results.

In addition to always learning more, expert traders also make sure that they validate everything they learn to decrease their risk exposure. Taking action on a strategy or advice that has not been validated through additional research is not ideal as it means you could be acting on bad advice. Traders always double and triple-check their research to ensure that they have access to the best new advice in their trades at all times.

Keeping a Trade Journal

Keeping a trade journal is a major point of opportunity when it comes to keeping yourself organized and following trends or patterns in the market. Expert traders use trade journals for just about everything, and they keep them for years after so that they can reflect on their notes at any given time. In fact, many expert traders even make a point of regularly reflecting back on their notes to see if there was any area they missed that they may be able to improve on in future trades.

As a trader, you should seek to keep plenty of journals on hand so that you can always document everything and keep those documents organized. I personally have four journals: one for tracking general stocks and creating my watchlists, one for technical analysis and notes on trade plans and executions, one for reviewing my processes, and one for writing down any additional notes I have. By keeping track of everything, I ensure that I am always in the position of keeping myself organized and keeping access to all of the best information possible.

I suggest that you keep all of these journals and keep extra on hand in case you need to start a new one for a new topic. Keep yourself organized with your journals by creating your own method for organizing your thoughts and notes so that everything makes sense to you. This way, you can always access historical notes, thoughts, or experiences to gain insight on how you might be able to improve present and future trade deals.

Validating Your Plans

Good traders make plans before every trade they enter to ensure that they are always making the best possible moves in the market. *Great* traders do not just make plans; they validate them against their own notes, additional research, and other people's experiences to ensure that they have the best plans possible. Great traders know that getting involved in a trade deal can be stressful, and they want access to the best possible strategy before they go in so that they can execute their trades to the highest profits possible.

Remember that you never want to pivot or change a strategy once you are invested in a trade, so you need to make sure that you have the best strategy possible before going into your trade. This means you need to have your risk tolerance and maximum loss identified and validated as being a strong position, and you need to have your target profit made so that you know when to exit the market with your profits. You also need to outline how and when you are going to manage the trade, so you know exactly how often to check-in without being obsessive or unnecessarily stirring up stress inside yourself.

In addition to having strong plans, expert traders will also make sure that they follow those plans at every single step of the process. Regardless of whether following the strategy will lead to a profit or a loss, they will follow it exactly to ensure that they follow through properly. Then, they will reflect on their trade to see if there was anything they could have done better to make the trade less stressful, more profitable, or less risky when it comes to losses, depending on how the trade played out.

Learning From Others

When you are trading, everyone else who is involved in trades is considered your competition. All of these people are investing in the same market as you and behaving in ways that you hope will result in you being able to take advantage of positions that will earn you more profits. For example, all of the other traders in the market are responsible for the prices rising and falling, which leads to you being able to take advantage of the positions that become available for you to profit from.

An expert trader sees these individuals as competition, but they do not separate themselves entirely from the competition. By that, I mean, they know that the competition is going to have great information that they can take advantage of to help them improve their own trade strategies and earn higher profits. For that reason, every single expert trader will always seek to learn more from others so that they can gain profits from their trades.

Expert traders will regularly pay attention to other peoples' behaviors in the market, join networking groups with other expert traders whom they can learn from, and share with others to learn and grow more. Their goal is never to give away their best trade secrets but to gain access to everyone else's as much as possible so that they can increase their own profitability and become even more successful in the stock market.

Regularly Cashing Out

Cashing out and taking your profits is part of being a trader. Beginners have a tendency to get greedy when they realize that the amount of money they have invested directly corresponds to the amount of money that they can make. By investing more money, they can make more money. While it is important to invest some of your profits back into the investments you are making so that you can profit even more from future trades, it would be naïve of you to invest everything back into future trades. Should you experience a loss at that point, you will lose everything and be back at zero.

Expert traders tend to follow the 30/70 rule, although they may adjust this ratio, depending on what their goals are and how soon they want to experience those goals in reality. The 30/70 rule indicates that a trader should cash out 30% of their profits while investing 70% back into the market. So, if the trader earned $100, they would keep $30 and invest $70 into a future trade.

Keeping part of your profits helps you feel the tangible benefits of your trades, which makes trading much easier. This way, you stay focused, and your losses do not feel as catastrophic because you have protected some of your funds by putting them into your bank account instead. These profits can then be applied toward actively living out your goals, such as quitting your job, traveling, or anything else you had laid out for yourself.

Taking Breaks and Having Fun

If you have ever looked at a group of professional traders, you will know that they are the ones that are most likely to let loose and have the most fun in social settings. They are known for thoroughly enjoying themselves and having uncapped levels of fun in their downtimes when they are not trading. The reason for this is that completely letting go, taking breaks, and having serious fun in between trades helps minimize the level of stress that you are experiencing from trades. This way, you are not experiencing ongoing residual stress from your trade day, and instead, you are able to move forward and go into your next trade day more relaxed and ready to focus.

Another benefit you get from taking breaks and having fun is the experience of celebrating yourself and your wins in the market. When you take breaks and have fun, such as by using some of your profits to attend a concert or go out for a nice dinner every once in a while, you get to *feel* the success you are creating. This, in turn, builds up your confidence and helps you feel even better about your ability to trade successfully. As a result, you are more likely to increase your trade skills and earn more from your trades going forward.

You do not need to start partying or spending every weekend going to fancy dinners. You only need to make sure that after each trade day, you reward yourself by taking the time to enjoy yourself to release the stress of trading from your mind and set yourself up for even more success.

Conclusion

Are you feeling like an expert trader yet? Or are you still feeling somewhat intimidated by the task of swing trading options?

Either answer is completely fine, especially knowing that you have access to the best possible resource that you could have as a beginner trader. You will find that by following the guidance I have provided you here and putting these techniques to work in actual trades, you will feel a lot more confident in what you have learned. The more you practice, the more confident you will feel, and the more success you will earn in your trade deals.

A large part of becoming a successful trader is getting involved in trades and seeing those trades through. By following this guidance and actively engaging in the entire step-by-step process, you will find that it becomes more familiar to you each time while also improving your skills. This way, you are able to create a stronger sense of confidence in yourself and in your trades. You will also be able to start accumulating your own research and knowledge around how these deals work so that you can apply your own understanding going forward. As a result, your trades will get even better.

Before you start engaging in actual trades, however, I strongly encourage you to engage in "practice trades." Practice trades are a strategy that many new traders use as an opportunity to get comfortable with trading before they actually invest any money into their trades. In fact, many expert traders will use practice trades as an opportunity to practice identifying good trade moves for new strategies before they actually execute a strategy. Practice trades are essentially trades that you engage in, where you act as if you were going to make a trade, but you never actually make the trade.

For example, if you want to practice swing trading, you would practice identifying the best possible positions for you to take in the market and then writing down in your practice journal at what point you would enter and what plan you would use. Then, you should practice managing that position as if you were actually already invested in it so that you can feel what that part of the trade feels like. Next, you should identify the exact moment at which you would exit the trade and why you would exit at that moment. Also, write down what profits or losses you would have experienced from your choices. Lastly, you should review your practice trade just like you would a real trade so that you know exactly where you did great and where you could have done better.

By executing a few practice trades before actually getting started with real trades using new strategies, you can build your confidence and increase your ability to execute strong trades going forward. I highly recommend this strategy to help you make the best possible trades. It may take longer for you to get started, but the experience and confidence you gain will help greatly in getting you to your goals when you start executing real trades.

When you begin executing real trades, make sure you keep this book handy, so you can refer back to it to help you make better trades. Also, make sure that you are conducting additional research at all times to validate everything you learn. This will ensure that everything you do is to the best of your understanding, which will minimize your risks and increase your profits. If you follow these techniques, you will have a great shot at making a huge profit in the stocks.

Lastly, before you go, I ask that you, please, take a moment to review *Swing Trading Options* on Amazon Kindle. Your honest feedback would be greatly appreciated and will help me make more great guides for you in the future.

Thank you and best of luck in reaching your financial goals by swing trading options!

Terminology

Call Option

A call option is a type of financial instrument that affords buyers the right to buy 100 shares at a pre-determined price, known as the strike price. In a call option, the seller is obligated to sell the stock, whereas the buyer has the option to buy the stock.

Exercise

Exercise means that the individual who has bought the option chooses to invoke the option, exercising their right to either buy or sell their shares at the strike price.

Expiration Date

Each option is written with an expiry date that outlines when the option must be exercised by. If the option is not exercised by the expiry date, the option expires worthless, meaning it was never exercised, and now, the option is no longer available.

Hedging

Hedging is a strategy used to reduce the risk of an investment by implementing a transaction that is used to offset the risk of the existing position.

Intrinsic Value

Intrinsic value is the value of an option that reflects the amount of profit that can be earned by that option. If an option is in the money, the intrinsic value is the market value minus the strike price. For example, if the market value of a stock is $50, and the strike price is $35, the intrinsic value of that stock is $15.

Long

Long is a term that is used to refer to a trader who is holding a long outlook on the market. Long positions, for example, are trade positions that will be held for weeks, months, or even years.

Premium

Premium is the value of the option contract itself. When you want to buy an option, the premium is what you will pay to purchase the contract from the seller.

Put Option

A put option is a type of financial instrument that affords buyers of the contract the right to sell 100 shares at the strike price on or before the expiry date of the option. With a put option, the contract buyer has the option to sell the stock, and the contract seller has an obligation to buy it.

Short

Short refers to a positional phrase. When someone is trading a short position, they are trading on a short pattern with the intention of gaining profits within a few hours or days, up to a week.

Strike Price

The strike price is the price of a stock in an option. The strike price is determined at the time the option is written and identifies how much the option buyer has the right to buy or sell their stock if they choose to exercise their option. For example, if the strike price is $50 and the stock increases to $75 value, the option holder can exercise their right to buy and acquire the stock at $50, undercutting market value by $25.

Time Decay

Time decay is a term that reflects the decaying value of an option that naturally takes place when the option starts to get closer to its expiry date. The closer the expiry comes, the less valuable the contract becomes.

Time Value

Time value is a term that reflects the value of a large amount of time left on an option contract. Options whose expiry dates are still a long distance away will cost more because you are securing a longer amount of time for a certain strike price.

Disclaimer

Swing Trading Options was written as an educational resource for individuals who are seeking to learn how to begin swing trading the options market. This book contains a large amount of material regarding the market that should be seen as educational material, only. This book does not guarantee results if the trader chooses to follow the materials written in this book. The author, publisher, and anyone else relating to this book do not assume any responsibility or liability for anyone's success or failure in trading through the use of this book. The results that the reader gains are their responsibility and theirs alone.

My FREE Gift for You

If you buy my other title, "*Swing Trading for Beginners,*" I will give you the 2 "Swing Trading" Audiobooks 100% FREE! Swing Trading for Beginners is an excellent title that teaches you all about how you can trade stocks using the Swing Trading Strategy. In that book, I go far deeper into the explanation of what swing trading is, how it works, and how you can trade any financial instrument using swing trading. It is an excellent resource to use, in addition to this book, to improve your trading skills and maximize your profits.

What Should I Read Next?

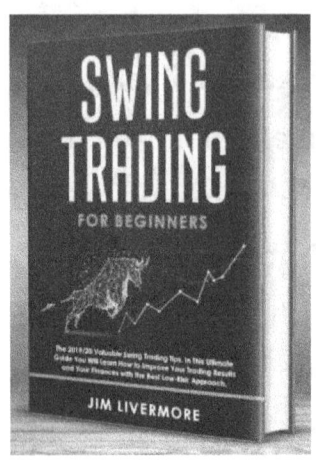

Swing Trading for Beginners: The 2019/20 Valuable Swing Trading Guide for Learning How to Improve Your Trading Results and Your Finances with the Best Low-Risk Approaches

Stocks Option Trading: Learn and Understand How Everything Works and What Pitfalls you MUST Avoid as a Beginner. Learn How Top Investors Lower Their Cost Basis Using Stock Options

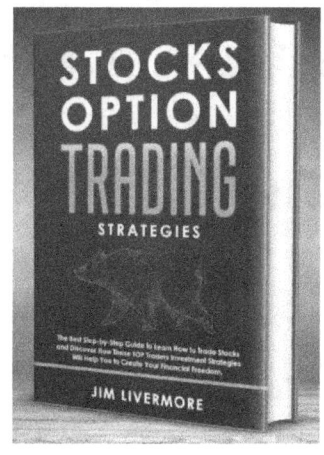

Stock Options Trading Strategies: The Best Step-by-Step Guide to Learn How to Trade Stocks and Discover How TOP Traders Invest. The Best Strategies to Help You Create Your Financial Freedom

Forex trading strategy: How to Invest with the Most Profitable and Simple Strategies to Make Money Trading Stocks, Options, Forex, Etfs in 2019 / 2020 Working Just 30 Minutes per Day.

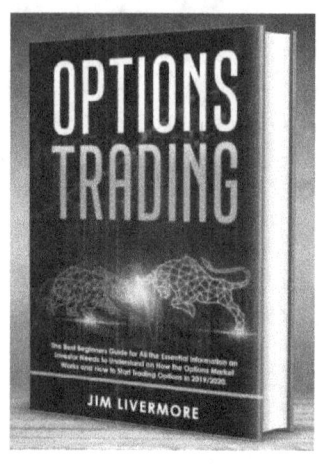

Options Trading: The Best Beginner's Guide with All the Essential Information an Investor Needs on How the Options Market Works and How to Start Trading Options in 2019/2020.